INSTRUCTIONS
ON THE ATONEMENT

INSTRUCTIONS
ON THE ATONEMENT

BY

PAUL B. BULL, M.A.

PRIEST OF THE COMMUNITY OF THE RESURRECTION,
MIRFIELD

LONGMANS, GREEN AND CO.
39 PATERNOSTER ROW, LONDON
FOURTH AVENUE & 30TH STREET, NEW YORK
BOMBAY, CALCUTTA AND MADRAS
1916

PREFACE

THIS book is a full expansion of some addresses given in St. Paul's Cathedral, London, in Lent, 1914. I have not attempted to alter their form entirely, or tried to eliminate appeals or exhortations which are more suited to sermons than to theological instruction. My conviction is that the Atonement is a subject so personal and intimate that it demands something more than the cold treatment of scientific theology. I have tried in this book to treat the subject from the point of view of the experience of life and love, and to urge the duty of keeping the whole process of the Atonement in view lest we lose the proportion of the Faith. I am in full sympathy with those Scottish theologians[1] who have reminded us that the death of Christ upon the Cross is the central crisis of the Atonement. There was much need to recall us to this truth. But to use the word "Atonement" only for this central action of a great process seems to risk a loss of proportion in the Faith, to forget that, as we are reconciled by Christ's death, so we are "saved by His life," and to narrow the appeal of the Catholic Church to men of one temperament and of one kind of spiritual experience.

The light of revelation shone through other minds besides St. Paul's; and the Catholic Church needs every

[1] Doctors J. G. Simpson, J. Denney, and P. T. Forsyth.

aspect of the truth if it is to embrace men of every temperament, and if every tribe and nation and kindred and people are to worship before the throne of God and of the Lamb.

I hope readers of this little book will correct the many imperfections of its outlook by reading also Dr. J. G. Simpson's "What is the Gospel?" and Moberly's "Atonement and Personality," two books from which I have derived the greatest spiritual benefit.

It only remains for me to thank Father G. W. Hart for generous labours in correcting the proofs; and to say that, if there is anything in these pages which is contrary to the Catholic Faith, I would wish it withdrawn.

Paul B. Bull, C.R.

The Priory of the Resurrection,
    77, Westbourne Terrace,
       London, W.
         Christmas, 1915.

TABLE OF CONTENTS

CHAPTER I

THE NEED OF THE ATONEMENT

PAGE

1. The Need of Penitence 1
2. The Nature of Sin 6
   i. Definition of Sin 7
   ii. Three Kinds of Sin : Venial, Mortal, and
   Sins of Omission 9
3. The Consequences of Sin 11
   i. Self-will and the Will of God . . . 11
   ii. Sin separates the Soul from God . . 13
   iii. Sin ends in Hell 16
4. Is Forgiveness Possible ? 20

CHAPTER II

THE GOSPEL OF IDENTIFICATION

1. Experience, not Explanation 24
2. False Notions of Atonement 26
3. The Catholic Doctrine of the Fall . . . 29
4. Atonement, Supernatural and Co-operative . 31
5. The Process of Atonement 32

CHAPTER III

THE INCARNATION

1. The Virgin Birth 35
2. The Temporal and the Eternal 36

PAGE

3. The Word became Flesh 38
4. The Method of the Incarnation 40
5. The Meaning of Sacrifice 43

CHAPTER IV

THE PASSION OF CHRIST

1. The Person and Work of Satan 48
    i. In the Writings of St. Paul and St. John . 51
    ii. In our Lord's Witness 53
2. The Unity and Solidarity in the Spirit-world . 54
3. The Passion is Timeless 56
4. The Passion, a Present Reality 57
5. Concurrent Processes. 59

CHAPTER V

THE DEATH OF CHRIST

1. The Friend of Sinners 61
2. A Voluntary Death 62
3. Gethsemane 64
4. Cases of Corporate Responsibility . . . 65
    i. The Family 66
    ii. The Nation 67
    iii. The Race 67
    iv. The Messiah 68
5. Cases of Death 69
    i. An event 69
    ii. Accidental Death 69
    iii. Sacrificial Death 70
    iv. Death for a Cause 70
    v. A Soldier's Death 71
    vi. A Martyr's Death 72
6. The Messiah's Death 72

CHAPTER VI

THE LIVING CHRIST

PAGE

1. The Lamb of God 79
2. The Ascension 80
3. The Cross Central, but not Exclusive . . . 82
4. Salvation, primarily Corporate 83
    i. The Bible 84
    ii. The Holy Catholic Church . . . 85

CHAPTER VII

MAN'S RESPONSE

1. Repentance 92
    i. Conviction of Sin, and Contrition . . 93
    ii. Conversion 94
    iii. What Sin costs God 95
    iv. Detachment and Attachment . . . 98
    v. Confession and Absolution . . . 100
2. Faith 104
    i. Trust and Self-surrender . . . 104
    ii. Re-creation 106
3. Strength 108
4. The Holy Spirit 109

CHAPTER VIII

THE REUNION OF CHRISTENDOM

1. Our Lord's Prayer 115
2. Reunion with the Church Expectant . . . 116
3. The Catholic Ideal 120
4. Varying Planes of Thought 122

BOOKS ON THE ATONEMENT

"Atonement and Personality." Moberly. 1901. (J. Murray.)

"What is the Gospel?" Dr. J. G. Simpson. 1914. (Longmans.)

"The Death of Christ." Dr. J. Denney. 1893. (Hodder and Stoughton.)

"The Atonement and the Modern Mind." Dr. J. Denney. 1903. (Hodder and Stoughton.)

"The Catholic Doctrine of the Atonement." H. N. Oxenham. 1865. (Longmans, Green.)

"The Cruciality of the Cross." Dr. P. T. Forsyth. (Hodder and Stoughton.)

"The Atonement." R. W. Dale. 1875. (Hodder and Stoughton.)

"Some Aspects of Sin." Aubrey Moore. 1891.

"Commentary on Epistle to the Romans." Bishop Gore. 1900. (J. Murray.)

"The Atonement." MacLeod Campbell. 1856.

"The Love of the Atonement." Milman. 1875. (Masters and Co.)

"The Ascended Christ." Professor Swete. 1911. (Macmillan.)

"The Christian Church." Darwell Stone. 1905. (Rivingtons.)

"The Church of Christ." E. Tyrrell Green. 1902. (Methuen.)

that all ethical progress has been won by resistance to the cosmic process. In this upward striving to be other than we are lies the first principle of Penitence; and in this resistance to the cosmic process is found the first indication of man's divine destiny, the instinct to fulfil the divine command to subdue the earth and have dominion over it (Gen. i. 28). This dissatisfaction with things as they are is the witness of the presence and power of an ideal; and it is this capacity for devotion to an ideal which chiefly differentiates man from the animals. This consciousness of an ideal, of a glimpse of the Heavenly Vision, this power to sit in judgment upon ourselves and to condemn ourselves when we fall short of our ideal;—is it not in this that man proclaims at once his glory and his shame —the glory of one who is made in the image of God, and the shame of one who has defiled or defaced that image?

This truth has been brought home to us picturesquely by a writer in some such words as these : " Man is an animal with an ideal. You won't understand what that means. Let me explain. If I see a man doing what is wrong or disgraceful, I pat him on the shoulder and say, ' Come, come, be a man, remember your manhood ! ' But if I were to see a monkey doing exactly the same things, I should not pat him on the shoulder and say, ' Come, come, be a monkey, remember your monkeyhood ! ' " Why this difference ? Because a man has an ideal, a glimpse of the Heavenly Vision of what he ought to be, and is capable of self-condemnation when he falls short of his ideal ; while, so far as we know, a monkey has no such ideal up to which he must strive to live. Is not this both the pain and the joy, the cross and the crown of every priesthood, of the saint, the artist, and the scholar ? Each one has seen a glimpse of the Heavenly Vision,— the Good, the Beautiful, the True ; and he agonizes

until he can give birth to the immortal thought with
which his soul is aflame.   And, in so far as he is a true
artist, he must love and suffer in giving birth to his vision.
He must endure the birth pangs—the joy of conception,
the aching longing to be delivered, the ineffectual efforts,
the failures, and the stern self-condemnation of what is
imperfect.

An art which is painless will also be worthless ; and
men who do not trouble their heads about their sins do
not know the birth of the divine within them.   The man
who is entirely satisfied with himself and his work has lost
the Heavenly Vision and the spring of progress.   He has
struck an equilibrium with his environment and so become
stagnant.   A nation which does not know how to be
penitent is decadent, unnerved by prosperity, soft, self-
indulgent, self-satisfied, and doomed to decay.

Surely it is the weak spot in the Superman of modern
philosophy that in his pride he is incapable of penitence,
and therefore of progress ; while the Supermen of the
Gospel, the twice-born sons of God, know the agony of
penitence as Christ is born within them and they are
gradually conformed to His Image.

It is one of the tragedies of life that men who were
capable of the sublime are content with mediocrity because they lack the courage of penitence, seek a painless
Christianity, acquiesce in faults of character, and are
content with a low level of attainment.

Compare the self-satisfied soul of the man who does
not trouble about his sins with the passion of a Christian
as seen in St. Paul.

> " Never at even, pillowed on a pleasure,
>   Sleep with the wings of aspiration furled,
>   Hide the last mite of the forbidden treasure,
>   Keep for my joys a world within a world,—

> Nay but much rather let me late returning
> Bruised of my brethren, wounded from within,
> Stoop with sad countenance and blushes burning,
> Bitter with weariness and sick with sin :—

> So to Thy presence get me and reveal it,
> Nothing ashamed of tears upon Thy Feet,
> Show the sore wound and beg Thine Hand to heal it,
> Pour Thee the bitter, pray Thee for the sweet."

There are only two bases on which to build our lives —Pride and Penitence.

Pride is man's estimate of himself as he appears in the eyes of men.

Penitence is man's estimate of himself as he appears in the sight of God.

Pride is in some cases the mother of barbaric virtues such as we cannot help admiring in Milton's fatally false picture of Satan in the "Paradise Lost," and a stimulant to high endeavour. It sometimes checks a man from what is shameful and impels him to what is noble. It gives him courage to shoulder responsibility. It gives force to decision and strength to resolve. It might be a virtue *if there were no God*. It is the highest virtue of the Superman, which enables him to dispute with Satan for the dominion of the world of illusion. But as soon as the sense of God dawns on man's vision, Pride is seen to be an illusion, and Penitence becomes the only true attitude of the soul. For God presents him with an ideal, a Heavenly Vision of what he ought to be : and, in the presence of that Heavenly Vision, truth compels a man to realize how far short of his ideal he has fallen, and to condemn himself in God's sight.

Pride is only possible so long as the eyes of the soul are blind to the vision of God. When man's eyes are open and he sees things as they really are, he becomes conscious of his imperfections—his sins.

It has been said that "when a monkey blushed, a man was born"; for the blush at once proclaims man's glory and his shame. It is the silent witness, the glowing revelation of a self-conscious personality. It reveals that man is conscious of an ideal and aware that he has fallen short of it; and that he has won the secret of Progress, the spirit of Penitence in which, in the full light of a lofty ideal, he has the courage to condemn himself. This courage of self-condemnation is the first step of an upward striving after perfection. Penitence delivers a man from that fatal self-satisfaction which condemns him to stagnation and robs him of all hope of high attainment.

Was it not a mistaken judgment which induced our leaders to depart from the traditions of the past and refuse a day of Humiliation at the beginning of the European War? We had nothing to repent of in our entrance on the war. God did not place before us an alternative: He gave us a command. But if we as a nation had had a deeper sense of our national sins, our luxury, our self-indulgence, our covetousness, our slavery to drink, our disintegrating individualism, our wilful self-assertion, our inefficiency, our unfitness for the holy task which God had placed upon us, we might have been spared some of the long-drawn days of humiliation which have humbled the pride of England and laid it bleeding in the dust.

Again, is it not just this lack of penitence, just this self-satisfaction of pride, just the spirit which refuses to trouble its head about its sins, which makes it so difficult to awaken Englishmen to the need of social reform? Hence it is that selfishness destroys brotherhood and pride embitters class hatred almost to the point of revolution.

Again, is it not pride on one side and on the other which has split Christendom into warring fragments, and paralysed its witness to the world? And the only hope of reunion lies in an ever-deepening penitence, which refuses the cheap methods of ignoring sin and of pretending that we who are divided are at one, and seeks to remove the cause of division by the humble and contrite confession of our sin.

2. The Nature of Sin

Perhaps the lack of the spirit of penitence and the dull weight of the religious indifference which oppressed England before the war were chiefly due to ignorance of the true nature of sin. And if we are to appreciate the full splendour of God's mercy in the Atonement, it can only be in so far as our conscience is quickened into a full realization of our sins and their consequences. There is no redemption for the Pharisee till he ceases to be one, until he can smite his breast with the Publican and cry " God be merciful to me a sinner." But at the present time many tendencies of our age help to blind men to the true hideousness of sin. The growth of towns which withdraws men from the witness of God in Nature, the spread of a shallow secular education which develops the intellect while it too often neglects to develop the conscience and the will, the excessive pressure of work which leaves men no time for reflection, the speeding up of life in every form which exhausts the inner forces of the soul in external activities, the softening of life which discountenances crimes of violence while it favours the development of more subtle forms of sin—all these help to account for a loss of conviction of sin, without encouraging the hope that the sin of our age is less than that of other ages. The world is more attractive, and therefore more dangerous. Vice is less gross, more subtle, and therefore less repellent and more destructive.

The witness of Christendom has been fatally weakened

by the competition of innumerable religious bodies which neutralize each other's work by making discipline impossible. This competition tends to lower the stern standards of the Gospel, and to substitute popular preaching for the rebuke of sin. The sting has gone out of the preaching of the Gospel, as Christians have made a compromise with the World. Religion has largely become a soporific which drugs the conscience, instead of a surgeon's knife which saves the soul. And without the conviction of sin there can be no conscious need of a Saviour.

So let us sketch out in brief outline the nature of sin and something of its guilt and its consequences.

(i.) *A Definition of Sin.*

What is Sin ? Sin is any failure or refusal to do the Will of God.

The whole basis of the Christian teaching about man is that he is a response. As the eye does not create the light, but the light plays upon those cells which are sensitive to its influence until the eye is formed and awakens to appreciate the light ; as the lungs do not create the air but respond to it ; so the soul does not create its God, but the power of God plays upon the soul of man until he becomes conscious of His influence, and responsive to His call. Beneath this inspiration man becomes gradually conscious of a power beyond himself, and it becomes possible for God to reveal, or unveil, Himself. And, in the presence of this unveiling of God, man becomes aware of his true nature and his divine destiny. He awakens to realize his dignity as made in the image of God by reason of his heart and mind and will. And with the realization of his freedom, his power of self-determination, comes the realization of his responsibility and of his sin.

It is obvious that a failure to respond to the will of God may be as deadly as a refusal. It is as possible to destroy one's life by starving it as by poisoning it. A lost opportunity may be as deadly as a misdirected action. We fail to hit a target as completely by not firing at it, as by missing it.

Man is often blinded by false standards of judgment. He persists in judging himself and others by the wrong done. But the Christian life is positive, not negative. Its aim is to do what is right, not merely to avoid what is wrong. Society condemns sins which are inconvenient to itself, which imperil its safety or comfort, or which shock respectability. But respectability is not holiness, and God does not accept the verdict of society. Society condemns theft and violence, but tolerates selfishness, covetousness, luxury, scandal, pride, and self-righteousness. Our Lord teaches that God reverses many human judgments, that the first shall be last and the last first, that the outcasts from society, the Publican and Harlot, will enter the Kingdom of God before the respectable self-righteous Pharisee (St. Matt. xxi. 31). He bids us see sin as God sees it, in its root in our hearts and minds and will. He drives us back from the outward action to the inward spirit, from the deed done to the motive which inspired it.

The root of all sin is Selfishness. From this root sin branches out into Covetousness, Pride, and Sensuality; or, to preserve the thought of selfishness as the essence of sin, we may call these branches Self-love, Self-assertion, and Self-indulgence. The essence of sin is to erect the human will into a separate centre of originality apart from God. Man's nature is to respond to God. Man's sin is to fail or to refuse to respond.

(ii.) *Three Kinds of Sin.*

We can roughly discern three classes of sins : Venial Sin, Mortal Sin, and Sins of Omission.

(*a*). *Venial Sin* is a sin of weakness. St. John teaches us that "there is a sin not unto death" (1 St. John v. 16). Again and again we do not deliberately intend to do what is wrong. But we are taken by surprise when we are off our guard, or the effect of past habits has weakened our self-control ; and the thought is tolerated, or the word is spoken, or the deed is done which our conscience at once condemns as sinful. Venial sin cannot be treated as in the same category with mortal or deadly sin, because it does not bear with it the same impulse of our will. But if it is lightly regarded, if we do not learn to hate it and try to conquer it, it may spread like a weed until it chokes all the avenues of the soul. A slight cold neglected may lead to more deep-seated evil. The grains of dust, too minute to be detected, may accumulate on the works of a watch until they stop its movement. The particles of salt may accumulate on the glass of a telescope until they blur it. So venial sin, if it is allowed to accumulate upon the soul, may rob it of its spring and joy, may hinder its activity and blind it to the Heavenly Vision.

(*b*). *Mortal Sin.* But we can detect a more grievous development of sin when the will deliberately sets itself in opposition to the Will of God, and refuses to obey His Voice. This class of sin is very terrible, as it definitely cuts the soul off from God, and breaks away from that communion with Him which is our eternal life. This sin does not always take the form of a deliberate rebellion. It is more often the subtle growth of a state or condition of the soul which gradually alienates the soul from union with the Heart and Mind and Will of God. So selfishness, or pride, or envy may grow unobserved until they have poisoned every activity of the soul and perverted our judgment so that at last we awake to find ourselves in a state of alienation from the life of God,—a soul which is dying, if not dead.

(c). *Sins of Omission.* Crossing these two divisions of sin on a different plane, we note that sins may be either sins of Commission, or sins of Omission. We have already seen that it is as easy to destroy life by starving it as it is by poisoning it. It is most important to note that in every parable of judgment the lost are lost not for what they have done but for what they have left undone or failed to do. The man is cast out from the marriage feast into outer darkness because he had not on the wedding garment which could have been had for the asking (St. Matt. xxii. 2–14). The Virgins found that the door was shut and heard the awful words "Depart from Me," because they had neglected, through sloth and procrastination, to provide themselves with oil for their lamps (St. Matt. xxv. 1–13). The servant was condemned because he had failed to make the most of the talent entrusted to him, and from cautious timidity had lost his opportunity (*ibid.* 14–30). Those on the left hand on the Day of Judgment who will hear the awful words, "Depart from Me, ye cursed, into the eternal fire," are condemned for the neglect of social service to the sick and poor and starving. "Inasmuch as ye did it not unto one of these least, ye did it not unto Me" (*ibid.* 45). And when we see so many professedly religious persons utterly indifferent to, even persistently opposed to, social reform which would relieve the awful burdens of the poor, so many churches which have become nests of Pharisees, absorbed in trivialities while they neglect righteousness, justice, and mercy, we tremble for that judgment which will begin in the sanctuary, and will shrivel up with eyes of flame those souls and nations which have neglected brotherhood and social service. Again, in the debtor who failed to forgive (St. Matt. xviii. 23–35), and in the fig-tree which produced no fruit (St. Luke xiii. 6–9), every parable of judgment warns us that God does not accept the verdict of society, but will judge us by our lost opportunities, our sins of omission. It was not the drunkard or the harlot who crucified the Son of God on Calvary, but the professedly religious people, the Pharisees blinded by pride and prejudice.

The sins which came under our Lord's most scathing condemnation were not those sins of violence or sensuality which society so readily condemns, but those subtler spiritual sins of selfishness and sloth, of pride and prejudice, of covetousness and luxury which society so readily condones.

This outline sketch of sin as we know it in experience will enable us to learn its essential nature and its eternal consequences.

3. The Consequences of Sin

(i.) *Self-will and the Will of God.*

We have seen that the essence of sin is selfishness. Sin sets up the human will as an independent centre of originality apart from God : and the consequence of sin is separation from God. " Your iniquities have separated between you and your God " (Is. lix. 2).

Of course we cannot fathom the dark mystery of evil. We can only faintly discern some of its movements, and analyse some of its effects. But though the mystery cannot be solved, the fact cannot be challenged. Sin is an awful reality to which every word of moral freedom bears unceasing testimony. Philosophers may discuss the age-long problem of determinism, and whether and how far man is responsible for his actions ; but in actual life the fact of freedom, self-determination and responsibility is unquestioned. We clearly recognize that at a certain point a person is not responsible for his actions, and for his own sake we place him under restraint in a lunatic asylum. As long as man uses the language of freedom and speaks of right and wrong, of conscience and of duty, as long as man is sufficiently noble to say, " I ought " and " I will," he proclaims his freedom and responsibility.

It is asked sometimes, " God is Almighty. All things were created by Him and exist only by His Will. Did God create sin ? " The answer to this question may be summarized thus. God might have peopled the world with automatic machines, with creatures as incapable of sinning as the stars on their courses. But in that case these creatures, moving under the iron rule of necessity, while incapable of sin would also be incapable of love. For love is free. It implies a choice, a self-determined movement of the will. Therefore, if God willed to create a being capable of responsive love, He must of necessity bestow that freedom without which love is impossible. In bestowing this freedom upon man, in sharing this divine prerogative with His creature, God placed a limit upon Himself.

In creating a being capable of responsive love He, of necessity, created one capable of refusing that response, and of withholding that love.

But it may be said, " If all things are created by the Will of God, then is not sin due to the Will of God ? "

No : for sin is not a thing : it is the perversion of a thing, the misdirection of a power. And may we not discern a distinction in God's Will ?   May we not say that some things are according to God's Will of *permission*, but not according to God's Will of *design?*   In the Parable of the Prodigal Son, the father might have prevented his son from going into the far-off country.   He might have robbed him of his freedom, locked him in the cellar, and forced him to stay at home.   But then he could not have claimed his love ; for love is of necessity free.   When the son gathered all together and went into the far-off country, it would be true to say that this was according to the father's will of permission ; but no one would suggest that it was according to his will of design. So with the possibility of sin.   Without the possibility of a wrong choice there can be no choice at all.   Therefore it seems true to say that sin is according to God's will of permission, but not according to His will of design. He allows it to exist ; and He overrules it to the ultimate fulfilment of His purpose.   So, because we have the awful responsibility of self-determination, it is always possible for us to rebel against God, and to convert our will into a separate centre of originality, apart from, and in many cases opposed to, the will of God.

(ii.) *Sin separates the Soul from God.*

And in the word " separates " lies the very nature and the awful consequences of sin.   " Your iniquities have separated between you and your God."   All sin, in its degree, separates from God.   Whatever separates from God is sin.   God is the life of the soul.   Sin is the disease and death of the soul.   Life in its every aspect is correspondence to its environment.   God is the environment of man.   " In Him we live, and move, and have our being " (Acts xvii. 28).

The sinful soul fails to correspond with the life of God,

and begins to perish. Just as when the lungs fail to correspond to the environment of the air, man's physical life begins to perish ; so, when the soul fails to correspond with the all-encompassing, all-pervading Presence of God, man's spiritual life begins to perish. The mind grows dull to spiritual things, and the Heavenly Vision gradually fades. The will grows weak in moral effort ; and it becomes more difficult to hear the Heavenly Voice. The heart grows cold to the movements of Divine Love, and tends to centre upon itself. A discord has occurred in the harmony of being. There has been a dislocation of essential relationships. Man is separated from the fountain of his being, from the source of his energy, from the spring of his life.

The outward life may go on for a time without betraying this discord, this dislocation. But it is there all the time, and makes itself felt in the loss of peace. There is, of course, a peace of indifference when a man does not trouble his head about his sins, when he has struck an equilibrium with his environment, and becomes stagnant on the lower level to which he has sunk ; when he acquiesces in faults of character and no longer strives upward toward an ideal. So the foolish virgins all slumbered and slept, indifferent to the Bridegroom's approach. So in Arctic regions the traveller feels an overwhelming desire to rest, and sleep entices him to yield to its fatal embrace. But all who love his life know that this is the coma which must inevitably end in death ; and they gladly inflict any suffering upon him to save him from this fatal sleep. So in many cases the surgeon's face blanches when the patient tells him that he no longer feels pain, because the surgeon knows that mortification has set in, and that the loss of sensation and the absence of pain means, not healing but, death. In contrast to this deadly peace of indifference is the peace of pardon which comes only with the pain of penitence, when the separation from God is healed, and the soul is restored again to union with Him Who is its life. This is the peace of harmony of being, of Atonement.

For the sin which separates us from God brings discord into the soul, so that a man is divided against himself. He knows the ceaseless conflict between his higher and his lower self, his conscience condemning what his heart desires, his lower will leading him to do what his higher self disapproves.

" For the good which I would I do not : but the evil which I would not, that I practise . . . for I delight in the law of God after the inward man, but I see a different law in my members, warring against the law of my mind, and bringing me into captivity under the law of sin, which is in my members. O wretched man that I am ! Who shall deliver me from the body of this death ? " (Rom. vii. 19–24).

So that sin which separates us from God throws our whole personality into discord. Unless we abandon the conflict in a cowardly spirit and forsake our ideal and acquiesce in sinking to a lower level of character, we shall value the pains of penitence as our only hope of salvation. The courage of Penitence is the only possibility of purification and of progress ; and we shall thank God for that preserving love which does not hesitate to inflict pain in order that He may save us from that peace of indifference, that coma which precedes the death of the soul. The pains of penitence are the evidence that the separation of the soul from God is not complete : they are the witness that the soul is yet alive.

" For the wages of sin is death " (Rom. vi. 23). " Then the lust, when it hath conceived, beareth sin : and the sin, when it is full grown, bringeth forth death" (St. James i. 15). The death of the soul is hell.

(iii.) *Sin ends in Hell.*

One of the greatest men of the last century has traced the collapse of morals and shallowness of character among young people in modern times to the failure of religious teachers to teach effectively about Hell. The result of this neglect is a kind of moral undenominationalism, a moral scepticism to which nothing is *very* right or wrong. This form of unbelief can make itself very popular with the multitude and wins the admiration of the world by treating sin as a phase of man's education, an undeveloped form of virtue, a regrettable error, and by indicating that it will all come right in the end, and that " to know all is to pardon all." It is such teaching as this which drugs souls into moral apathy, and robs the Gospel of its all-saving power.

It is most painful to speak of Hell, but it is most perilous to be silent ; for many souls come to utter ruin because they do not realize the destructive effect of sin, and the possibility of final loss. It is to be noticed that the most terrible warning against the destructive effect of sin comes not from the writings of the Apostles, but from the lips of our Lord Himself. We cannot then dismiss the thought of Hell as inconsistent with the love and mercy of God. For it is from those very lips which have taught us God's love and mercy that we hear the stern and awful truth that sin reaches its final consummation in that state " where their worm dieth not, and the fire is not quenched " (St. Mark ix. 48; see St. Matt. xviii. 6, etc.). No doubt much of the disregard of this stern aspect of our Lord's teaching is due to a wholesome reaction against the crude Calvinistic doctrine that God foreordains some souls to eternal torment. But now that this repulsive teaching has been exposed as a slander against the character of God, we can see more clearly than ever the force of our Lord's warning. It is eternal Love which tells us that sin may destroy the soul in Hell. It is not true love, but the moral feebleness of a pleasure-loving age which fears to give a faithful echo to His teaching. In facing this awful truth, we must remember that God never sends anyone to Hell. God's will is that "all men should be saved and come to the knowledge of the truth" (1 Tim. ii. 4). There is no death for a soul but the death of spiritual suicide. God will part with no one who does not say to Him, face to face, "I will not have Thee."

Man makes his own hell in his own heart. Science tells us of a katabolic process as well as an anabolic, of a degradation of energy, of a process of running down, of a tendency of forces to sink down into inertia. Philosophy warns us of the tendency of habits to harden, and to become more fixed, as thoughts or words or deeds are constantly repeated. Experience tells us that sin often repeated does weaken the will, and blind the mind, and harden the heart. The destructive effect of sin on the soul may be likened to the action of sulphuric acid on the body. If a man drops vitriol on his eyeball, it is a mistake to say that God punishes him with blindness. The sulphuric acid destroys his instrument of sight and deprives him of his power to see. So every sin in its degree destroys in the soul something of its ability to see the Heavenly Vision, to hear the Heavenly Voice and eats out something of the capacity for love. Love is Heaven ; inability to love is Hell. Sin is selfishness ; and Hell is selfishness consummated. The selfish soul gradually destroys its capacity for loving others. Little by little it

c

hardens itself to their love, until it makes a loveless desert all around it, and has a foretaste of that isolation which is the eternal solitude of a lost soul.

This is a truth of experience, not merely a dogma of theology. Once a young man who had been given all that the world has to give in the way of opportunity, education, influence, wealth, and talents, and had squandered his life and health and strength in sin, after evading every effort I had made to help him, asked me in a flippant way, " I wonder why parsons don't preach more about Hell. When I was a boy, I heard of nothing but fire and brimstone. But now we seem too refined to mention it." I told him that I did not say much about Hell for two reasons. Firstly, because I believe that it begins in this life. Secondly, because a man knows it when he is in it. He turned round to me a white and haggard face and said, " I know it. I'm in it now." He went on to tell me of the fires which are not quenched, of the passions which he himself had kindled and inflamed and indulged until he had lost the power to gratify them. He said that his self-indulgence had destroyed his capacity to love, so that he could not even love his own mother who had once been the unselfish passion of his life.

Another young man who had wasted his opportunities of a good education, and had sunk to a lower level in the social scale came to me in an abiding state of deep depression. I pointed out to him that, if he had the courage, he might still form a splendid character in his present surroundings. He admitted this, but said with infinite sadness, " Ah, yes, but it gnaws me like a worm to think what I might have been." Does not experience then interpret the expressions which our Lord used when He warned men of " the worm " of remorse " which dieth not," and of those "fires " of passion "which never will be quenched " ?   In the cases quoted, sin had not yet been perfected ; the soul was still alive and, amidst the pains of penitence, found One Who could redeem, One Who could bridge the separation of sin and reunite the soul to God in His wonderful Atonement, One Who could restore again by creative love what had been destroyed by the craft and malice of the Devil, One Who could give back the years which the locust had eaten, and engrave again the image which had been marred.   But if we are to appreciate that great Atonement, we must have the courage to gaze with open eyes on sin in its ultimate issue as eternal Death, to know that it is a separation which may become final if the soul will not repent.

One word of warning.   We must, when we dare to meditate thus on Hell, apply the thought to ourselves alone, and not to others.   Too ready are we to forget the command, "Judge not that ye be not judged " (St. Matt. vii. 1).   For others, it is our duty to remember that all human judgment is of necessity fallacious, that man can only judge by the outward expression of the life, while God judges by the inward motive : that man sees the failure to win the victory, while God alone knows the strength of the temptation and the heroic, if ineffectual, efforts to resist it ; that man judges by results accomplished, God by efforts made. Anxiety about others who are dear to us will stimulate our efforts for their conversion ; but it must never quench our hope or silence our prayers on their behalf. Are you anxious for the soul whom you love and who perhaps has passed away without any sign of repentance or of faith ?   Remember then that God loves that soul more than you do, and will do all that can be done for it.   We must apply the thought of Hell to ourselves alone, and not to others.   This realization of Hell as eternal separation from God will deepen our hatred of sin and our gratitude for the Atonement.

So we may thus sum up the truths which we have so far touched upon. God is Love. Sin destroys our capacity for Love. Salvation is union with God. Sin is separation from God. Atonement is reunion with God. Heaven is Fellowship. Hell is isolation, selfishness consummated. To love is to live. Sin is separation from God. Separation from God allows the soul to fall into discord, disorder, and dissolution. Sin is the disease of the soul. Its effects are the waste of the energies of life and of life's opportunities, the famine of the heart, the slavery which degrades and robs the will of its freedom, the acid which eats away all the soul's power of vision and leaves it blind, the destruction of faith, the withering of hope so that the soul goes down and down through decay and dissolution to despair, the perishing of love which through selfishness decays into cynicism. Sin destroys the power to love. Therefore hate sin in its first movements. If we see the end, we shall avoid the beginning. And the end of sin is Hell.

4. Is Forgiveness Possible?

Having glanced at sin and its consequences in the disease and death of the soul, we may now appreciate the great and sublime mystery of the Atonement. But before we can rightly enter upon this, a word must be said as to the possibility of forgiveness. For many men to-day deny that forgiveness is possible. They are obsessed with that utterly discredited mechanical conception of the universe which regarded it as a machine, a " closed in " system in which various forces work out their inevitable destiny under the iron law of Necessity. Their point of view represents much truth, and is a useful corrective

to that frivolous moral scepticism which makes light of
sin with the assurance that it will all come right in the
end. The truth which they represent is the awful reality
of sin : the truth which they ignore is that the essential
nature of sin is a dislocation of personal relationship.
And this ignorance leads them to a wrong conclusion.
They say, " Why speak of forgiveness ? The word spoken
cannot be recalled. The deed done cannot be undone.
Facts are facts. As a man sows, so shall he reap. The
opportunity lost is a gap for ever whirling away on the
wings of the past. The deed done is caught up into the
network of cause and effect, and must work out its
inevitable consequences. Things are what they are."

Quite true so far as it goes ; but it does not go far
enough. Things are what they are : but persons are not
things. And sin is personal : it is the dislocation of
personal relationship.

Perhaps the fallacy of the argument against the possibility of forgiveness will best be seen if we distinguish
between the temporal and the eternal consequences of
sin. Sin involves two things ; (1) a thought nourished,
a word spoken, or deed done, and (2) the will to do it.

The temporal consequences enter into the mechanism
of time and space. The evil thought tolerated canalizes
the brain and affects the character. The word spoken
gives a body to the thought, and, riding on the waves of
the atmosphere, affects other minds and breeds new
thoughts. The deed done is caught up into the network
of cause and effect, of antecedent and consequent, which
make the woven web of history. These are the temporal
consequences which are caught up inextricably into the
mechanism of Time and Space and cannot be undone,
though their effect may be counteracted and overruled
and redirected. But the soul of a thought or word or

deed, that which gives it life and vitality, that which gives it moral value and makes it our own, is the *will* which stamps it with the signature of our personality. The evil thought which is not tolerated, but hated, loathed and despised, does not belong to us, does not bear our signature. It belongs to the devil who suggested it, and not to us who loathe it. But the evil thought which is tolerated breeds in the mind, and enters into our character. The word when it has passed our lips is our own creation. In varying degree it bears the signature of our will, and enters on its activity for good or evil in a way which is beyond our control. The deed done is done for ever. It enters into the mechanism of Time and Space, as far as its temporal consequences are concerned ; but its moral character depends upon its motive. This is recognized by law. When one man kills another, judge and jury have to try to discern the soul of the deed. Its temporal consequences are the same in either case. The man is dead, his wife a widow, his children fatherless ; but the moral value of the act depends on its soul, on the amount of will and intention which energized in the deed. If it is purely accidental there is no guilt; it is a case of accidental homicide. If the intention and will of the agent found expression in the act, then he is guilty of a crime. The temporal consequences are the same in both cases—the man is dead. But in accidental homicide there are no eternal consequences ; in murder there are. For in murder the act bears the signature of the will. The eternal consequences are that the man's will has been separated from the Will of God. Eternal does not mean duration in time, but relationship with God. To be united to God in heart and mind and will is Eternal Life. Separation from God means eternal death : and all sin in its degree separates us from God. The *temporal* consequences of sin cannot be undone : though God in His mercy often allows them to be overruled in such a way as to rob them of their virulence.   But our merciful Father has provided a way in which the *eternal* consequences of sin may be averted and undone.   " Neither doth God take away life, but deviseth means that he that is banished be not an outcast from Him " (2 Sam. xiv. 14).   Forgiveness of sin is possible because the essential nature of sin is that it is a dislocation of our personal relationship with God.

This means of restoration, this method of reunion, this mystery of the Atonement, this miracle of redeeming Love, must now engage our attention.

CHAPTER II

THE GOSPEL OF IDENTIFICATION

1. Experience, not Explanation

IN meditating on the great mystery of the Atonement,
it is well to remind ourselves that it is not in the
least necessary for us to have any theory as to how this
blessed fact is accomplished. The Holy Catholic Church
has no official explanation of the Atonement. She con-
tents herself with a statement of fact about it ; and this
fact that Christ reconciles us to God cannot be disputed.
It is a fact of experience to which millions of souls bear
witness, that in Him they have the forgiveness of their
sins and reconciliation with God. We should remember that inability to explain how a thing comes to pass,
or why it happens in such a way and not in some other
way, never affects in the least our belief in the fact itself.

The gunner who fires a shell with perfect accuracy
produces the same effect of destruction whether he
knows, or does not know, how that effect is accomplished.
He may be entirely ignorant of the nature of cordite,
melinite, or lyddite with which the shell is charged. He
may be quite unable to explain the " how " or the " why "
of those chemical changes and that burning of the fuse
which cause the shell to explode in a certain time. Of
course the more he understands of these, the more interesting his work becomes, and the less likely is he to make
mistakes if left to his own initiative. But if he trusts

and obeys those who teach him, the effect can be accomplished without his being able in any way to explain the " how " and the " why."

So a patient may be restored to health by medicine and treatment if he trusts his doctor and obeys, without any knowledge whatever of the ingredients of his medicine or of its action and reaction on the various parts of the body.

In fact it is one of the most interesting results of the philosophic criticism of science that scientific men now admit that they know absolutely nothing of the ultimate " how " and " why " of the universe. We live, but we know nothing whatever of the ultimate nature of life. We play about with matter and force, with ether and energy ; we observe that they act and react in a certain way ; and this knowledge enables us to combine and control them to some extent to the fulfilment of our will. We call this ordered sequence of antecedent and consequent the Laws of Nature. But we know nothing whatever of the ultimate nature of matter or force, of ether or energy. We know neither what they are, nor why they are what they are.

Modern science, in so far as it is truly scientific, adopts a humble attitude of reverent agnosticism as to the ultimate constitution of the Universe. And modern theology, in the presence of the still loftier mysteries of God and man's salvation, must adopt the same attitude of humble and reverent agnosticism as to the ultimate nature of many a Christian mystery. God has revealed to man enough truth to secure his salvation, but not enough to satisfy his curiosity.

So when we meditate on the mystery of the Atonement, it is well to remember that the knowledge of the fact that in Christ God bestows on us the forgiveness of our sins is entirely independent of our ability, or inability, to explain the process of reconciliation. And this reverent Christian agnosticism as to the " how " and " why " is especially necessary in dealing with the mystery of the Atonement. For we are dealing with three of the ultimate mysteries of the Universe, the Being of God, the Mystery of Evil, and the Nature of man,—three mysteries of light and of darkness and of shadow. We move amidst these mysteries knowing that by sin our own faculties have been disordered, and that therefore we cannot see clearly into the depths of the Divine Nature : knowing also that, though the image of God within us has been marred by sin, it has not been entirely destroyed. In the Fall man lost the supernatural grace by which he held communion with his Maker, and his natural faculties were disordered, wounded, and thrown into confusion ; but he still retains enough affinity with God to recognize the Divine when he sees it.

2. False Notions of Atonement

This divine instinct enables us to dismiss much of the teaching of the followers of Luther and Calvin on the Atonement as tending to false conclusions, or as grossly immoral in their ultimate issues, and to guide our thoughts on the Atonement by the twofold principle of the experience of life and the law of love.

The healthy moral instincts which still remain even in our sinful nature enable us to dismiss from our consideration the repulsive doctrines of some forms of Protestantism as to the total depravity of the human race, the absolute election of some to final salvation, the limitation of the Atonement to the elect, and the predestination of some to eternal damnation.

And with these repulsive doctrines we may dismiss those forensic discussions of the method of the Atonement which were drawn by legal minds from the methods of the Law Courts. The crude teaching of mere Substitution, by which an angry Father is said to have punished an innocent Son instead of the guilty sinner, while it still finds a place in the preaching of ignorant evangelists, does not commend itself to the wholesome moral instincts of mankind. And this doctrine of mere substitution is not only a slander on the character of God, but is also fatally injurious to the moral restoration of man. There is a Catholic doctrine of substitution which shows man encompassed and inter-penetrated and made one with the larger personality of Jesus, the Son of God. He does for us much, nay *all*, that we cannot do for ourselves. In this great margin of a larger and a sinless Humanity upon which we can draw by virtue of that Love of God which has made us one with Him, we find that Catholic doctrine of substitution which assures us that Christ does for us what we cannot do for ourselves. We may roughly say that Protestantism teaches that grace is imputed, while the Church teaches that grace is imparted ; that Protestantism teaches a doctrine of mere substitution, while the Church teaches the Gospel of Identification. The crude doctrine of mere substitution has become repulsive to many good men because, as it is frequently preached, it is degrading and immoral in its tendencies. As frequently preached, it glories in the escape from the punishment of sin which He suffered instead of us ; whereas every honourable man wishes to receive some punishment for sin, as far as he can bear it, provided he may be pardoned and restored. Vicarious suffering is an inevitable consequence of our solidarity as Family, Nation,

Race. Willingly borne, it exalts the bearer and purifies
the life of the whole ; but directly the eyes are taken
off the bearer and fastened on the escape, as in so much
preaching, the result is degrading. The man who allows
another to be punished for his sins and rejoices at his
own escape is a mean-spirited person, an immoral character. We should expect any good man to refuse to allow
such a thing, and to mourn for it if he could not prevent
it. Yet I have heard an eloquent canon move a vast
congregation to tears by a vivid description of Barabbas
with his wife and children, gazing at Christ hanging
dead upon the Cross and saying, "He died instead
of me." No suggestion was made that Barabbas had
been or was converted. The whole emphasis was on
his escape from the just penalty of sin ; and the sermon
seemed to me grossly immoral. There is also the
real danger that the doctrine "Christ instead of me"
may be, as indeed it is, frequently paraphrased thus :
"Christ suffered instead of me, therefore I need not
suffer." So from the degraded depths of a luxurious and
self-indulgent life men contemplate their Substitute with
gratitude to Him that He has borne the penalty of their
sins, and with a more fervent feeling of joy that they
themselves have escaped the necessity of suffering, and
can live in comfort and luxury. They forget the saying of
our Lord which teaches "identification" rather than
"substitution," viz. that no man can claim a share in the
merits of the Cross of Christ unless he too will deny himself and take up his cross daily and follow Him. We shall
never get rid of bejewelled, luxurious, self-indulgent
Christianity until "identification" is preached together
with the Catholic doctrine of substitution, viz. that Christ
did for us what we could not do for ourselves.

Dismissing the crude doctrines of mere substitution,

tary, but is certain, when uncontrolled by grace, to lead men into sin. ['Each man is tempted when he is drawn away by his own lust and enticed. Then lust, when it hath conceived, beareth sin, and sin, when it is full grown, bringeth forth death' (St. James i. 14, 15).] Freewill was impaired, but not destroyed at the Fall, and man was therefore able to co-operate with grace, when offered, but unable of himself to do any acts pleasing to God, and deserving eternal life. This deprivation of supernatural grace, with its moral and natural consequences, implying further the loss of his claim to supernatural beatitude, our first parent transmitted to his posterity; but not, of course, his personal guilt, or, as was strangely imagined by the Reformers, any positive evil quality; and they could only be restored by the merits of Christ to the state of grace which he had forfeited. Man cannot merit or obtain restoration for himself, but he can and must co-operate freely with the grace of God calling him to repentance, and this is sometimes termed in scholastic language 'merit of congruity.' On his true repentance he is forgiven, and with remission of sin the love of God is infused into his heart, and he is thus not only accounted, but made righteous, and enabled to do works pleasing to God and deserving eternal life. Justification and sanctification are different names for the same thing, accordingly as it is viewed in its origin or its nature, except that, in ordinary language, justification is used for the initial act on the part of God in a process of which sanctification, in its fullest sense, is the gradually accomplished result; they stand to each other in the spiritual life, as birth in the natural life to the gradual advance to maturity. The sinner is justified, not by a bare acquittal, or by some juridical fiction of a transfer of Christ's merits, as though they were his own,

but by the gift of inherent righteousness, or indwelling
of the Holy Ghost, bestowed (primarily in baptism) for
the merits of Christ. That gift though not *of* him is *in*
him, and he is thereby also sanctified, not in name but
in reality. Hence all merit, properly speaking, is ulti-
mately derived from that of the Redeemer, and in crowning our merits God crowns His own gifts."

4. ATONEMENT, SUPERNATURAL AND CO-OPERATIVE

We see from this statement of Catholic doctrine that
the Atonement must be at once supernatural and co-
operative. It comes from above. It works from within.
Man cannot accomplish it without God. God will not
accomplish it without man. What Christ does *for* us,
He must do *in* us. It must be supernatural, because by
no natural power can man reunite himself to God. It
must be supernatural because it is creative. Sin destroys,
and God must recreate in us what sin has destroyed. It
must be co-operative, because the free gift of God must
be received, and accepted, and assimilated. Man must
do whatever he is yet able to do to respond to the gift of
God. Just as the bestowal of food cannot repair the waste
of the body unless we assimilate the food and make it
our own; just as medicine can have no healing power
unless we absorb it into our system so that it becomes a
part of ourselves—so we must co-operate with God by
the response of Penitence and Faith, if the poison of sin
is to be purged from our hearts, and if the wounds and
diseases of our souls are to be healed.

It is this divine and supernatural creative act of God
by which He reunites man to Himself which we may now
consider under the title by which the process of the Atonement is best described—the Gospel of Identification.

5. The Process of Atonement

The meaning of Atonement is best understood by splitting the word up into its component parts, and writing it down as " At-one-ment." We see at once that the word stands for that majestic process of reunion by which God makes man " at one " with Himself. Sin separates man from God : God, in the Atonement, reunites man to Himself. The process of reunion, or " at-one-ment," is accomplished by an interpenetration which blends the life of God and man into one. As the life of the three Persons of the ever blessed Trinity is one in the Unity of the Godhead, and this Unity consists without either " confounding the Persons or dividing the substance," so God, without absorbing or destroying our personality, uplifts us, in spite of our sins, by a supreme Act of Love, into union with Himself. In that union with the life of God sin is destroyed and man is recreated. We should not dare to use this language of union, identification, interpenetration, if our Lord had not Himself first used it :— " I in them, and Thou in Me, that they may be perfected into One " (St. John xvii. 23).

The history of man in his relationship to God may be described by these words : Union—Separation—Reunion—Communion. These are the four words of the Atonement. And day by day the Church repeats them in word and deed. In word, the glorious process of the Atonement is commemorated three times a day, when at Matins, Eucharist, and Evensong we recite the Creed. For the Creed is the record of the Atonement as it was accomplished in history. But the Church brings the Atonement before us day by day not only in word, but also in deed. Although the divine action can never be repeated, it must always be continuous, as long as sin separates man from God. What God did on the stage of history for the human race is applied day by day to the individual soul in the Sacraments of the Church. The day begins by the pleading of the Holy Sacrifice in which Jesus our Great High Priest offers Himself to the Father, as the " full, perfect, and sufficient sacrifice, oblation, and satisfaction for the sins of the whole world."

In this sacred drama the whole process of the Atonement is re-presented, i.e. is presented again. The Eucharist is our Bethlehem, our House of Bread, in which, by the over-shadowing of the Holy Ghost, our bread and wine are caught up into union with the divine Humanity of our dear Redeemer and become His Body and Blood, so that the Word becomes Flesh and dwells amongst us. The Eucharist is our Calvary, where the Body is broken and the Blood outpoured for our redemption. The Eucharist is our Garden of the Resurrection, where Christ comes to us in His risen life to incorporate us into His divine Humanity. The Eucharist is our Mount of the Ascension where, incorporated into His risen life, we are caught up into Heavenly places in union with our ascended Lord, and presented by Him to the Father. The Holy Eucharist is our foretaste of Heaven wherein time and space fade away, and we move amidst Cherubim and Seraphim and all the hosts of saints and angels before the throne of God and of the Lamb.

But not only thus does the Church show forth day by day the great sublime process and mystery of the Atonement. As the little infant is brought to Holy Baptism, he is made " at one " with Christ, buried with Him in death, born again of water and of the Spirit by His creative act, receives the remission of his sins by spiritual regeneration, and is sanctified by the Holy Spirit.

D

As the penitent kneels to confess his sins which have in their degree separated him from God, he is restored again by Absolution to that full communion with God which is eternal life.

As the faithful communicant receives the Body and Blood of Jesus, he is made "at one" with Him, and is caught up body and soul in the power of that great Atonement into the embrace of God, so that God dwells in him and he in God.

Thus day by day the Catholic Church shows forth in word and deed that sublime action of the Atonement, that supernatural movement of God manward by which man is restored again by a new creative act of God to that communion which is Eternal Life.

But we shall not grasp the full and inexhaustible riches of God's grace and mercy in our redemption unless we accustom ourselves to the idea of concurrent processes. That Atonement which is wrought out under the conditions of time and space upon the stage of history is primarily historical ; but its fulfilment in history is not an isolated action, without antecedent or consequences. The historical facts of the Atonement are the manifestation in time of God's eternal will and purpose ; and we shall best realize the splendour of this divine action if we see it on the varying planes of thought. We dimly perceive that what God wrought in history may be contemplated on different planes of thought in its Cosmic, Historical, Mystical, Sacramental, and Ecclesiastical significance.

CHAPTER III

THE INCARNATION

1. THE VIRGIN BIRTH

THAT which most jars upon the minds of thoughtful men to-day, in the contemplation of such facts of the Christian Faith as the Virgin Birth, and the glorious Resurrection of our dear Redeemer, is the feeling that they come suddenly upon us as isolated freaks in an ordered series of events. This difficulty is in part quite unreasonable. It is due to the fact that such minds have unconsciously accepted a false conception of the Universe, the mechanical conception, which treats the Universe as a " closed-in " system, and resents the thought that God can influence His creation. This mechanical conception of the Universe is an illusion of those minds which have become obsessed by the methods of Science, and have lost their elasticity. As a cab-horse may become so much accustomed to running between shafts and along streets that he really no longer knows how to play about and enjoy himself in the open fields, so the mind which, with stern loyalty to one method of attaining truth, drills itself to run only between the shafts of logic loses something of its freedom and elasticity. Just as the German soldier, abandoning himself to the drill sergeant, loses the freedom and spontaneity of his personality, and becomes part of a vast machine, so the mind which is trained only in the barrack square of the scientific method misses the revelations of the personal which come to us in art, music, poetry, love, heroism, and religion, and too often abandons itself to the illusion of the mechanical. To such minds the Christian faith with its doctrine of the irruption of God into human affairs seems, as of course it does, to spoil the working of the machine and to shatter the mechanical conception of the Universe. We have tried to show else-where[1] that this mechanical conception of the Universe is an illusion which receives no support either from true Science or from Philosophy. In so far as this has been successfully demonstrated, we may dismiss as unreasonable this objection to the facts of the Christian faith.

But to other minds the same difficulty occurs when such facts as the Virgin Birth and the Resurrection seem to be isolated events which do not harmonize with the revelation of God's will in the ordered sequence of History. This difficulty is more reasonable. It is probably due to the controversial habit of discussing such facts apart from their context. When the Virgin Birth and Resurrection of our Lord are seen in their context as part of the great process of the Atonement, and when the historical fulfilment of the Atonement is seen as the manifestation in time and space of God's eternal purpose, then we may hope that this difficulty will be removed.

2. The Temporal and the Eternal

A person sitting on the top of a perfectly conical mountain sees at one glance a long procession of persons winding their way up to the summit. All, the first and the last, those who are highest and those who are lowest down, are present to him in one moment. But to those who are moving in the procession there is a necessary sequence. Some are going before, some following after:

[1] See *The Sacramental Principle*, pp. 9–32.

some are out of sight, hidden by the turn of the road :
some can be seen above or below them, winding their
way up the same path, and then they disappear from
sight, to reappear again.

So the Procession of the Ages, the past, the present
and the future, winds its way up the Mount of God. To
themselves they follow or precede one another ; to God
they are all present in the Eternal " Now."

So the Procession of Life winds its way up from primae-
val chaos ; and we may look at it from one of two points
of view, the Historical or the Eternal. We may take the
procession at any particular point, and see what precedes
and what follows. That is the Time Series. Or we may
see it as a whole as God sees it, in spiritual states rather
than in facts or things done. From this point of view we
may note the upward striving, the downward tendency,
the yearning aspiration, the ineffectual efforts on the
part of man : and the eternal Purpose, the all-embracing
Love, the encompassing Will, the inspiring strength on
the part of God.

Looked at as a whole, we see that the Atonement is
the eternal Purpose of God. As soon as sin becomes a
possibility, redemption becomes a purpose. The Lamb
" hath been slain from the foundation of the world "
(Rev. xiii. 8).

Looked at from the point of view of the Processions,
we see the human race sinful, weak, and wandering, unable in its own strength to accomplish the ascent, mis-
taking the path, blind, wilful, and perverse with misdirected will, bewildered, distracted, disheartened, growing
dull in aspiration, botanizing by the wayside, chasing
butterflies, its heart poisoned, its will weakened, its mind
blinded by sin, bound by the chains of habit, bewitched
and mesmerized by Satan. Then we see a majestic

movement of God, Who by Virgin Birth knits Himself into the very texture of the procession ; becomes one with us ; embraces man sick with sin ; sucks the poison of sin from our wound, absorbs it into Himself that it may lose its power to harm ; destroys it in the crisis on Calvary ; shatters the power of Satan ; rises from the dead ; withdraws at the Ascension from the limitations of Time and Space, not in order that He may forsake us, but in order that He may be always and everywhere present to all who desire Him.   And from that point we see the procession moving upward with quickened step, free from the chains which bound it, free from the mesmerism of Satan which enthralled it, restored to health and throbbing with the vigour of the life of God—the march of the Redeemed.   Having glanced at this vision as a whole, we may now proceed to examine it in detail.

3. The Word became Flesh

Sin separates man from God. The Atonement is that process by which God restores man to union with Himself, makes man " at one " with God.

In the Incarnation the Eternal Son of God lays aside the glory of His Godhead and takes our human nature into union with His Divine Person, making it " at one " with Himself. By a new creative act, as supernatural as the first creation, God re-creates our human nature by taking it into union with Himself. He knits Himself into union with the human race in order that He may knit us into union with His divine life. The Son of God becomes the Son of Man in order that the sons of men may become the sons of God. It is supernatural, for no forces of nature could accomplish it. It is co-operative, because God uses the purest and best flower of the human race as the source from which He draws the material of His manhood. All glory to that pure and undefiled Virgin who in her self-surrender offers to God the opportunity of the world's redemption, and in becoming the Mother of the Redeemer, becomes also the Mother of the Redeemed ! Our redemption comes from above by the overshadowing of the Holy Spirit ; it works from within by the co-operation of the Blessed Virgin Mary. The birth of the Son of God at Bethlehem, "conceived by the Holy Ghost, born of the Virgin Mary," is not an isolated fact, a thing done without antecedents or consequences. It is a consummation of the past, and the beginning of the future, indwelling of man by God.

The Eternal Word had always been the light that lighteth every man. Every dim discernment of the distinction between right and wrong, every movement of love, every holy aspiration, every blush of shame, every effort to do right—all these witness to the presence of God in the heart of man. But sin had blinded man to God's indwelling and to the Heavenly Vision. At the Incarnation He Who had always dwelt within man comes outside man, and moves across the stage of History in order that poor blinded man may see in terms which he cannot misunderstand, for they are his own, in the drama of a human life, the revelation of the love of God for man. As our personality finds self-expression when thought becomes incarnate in a word, and still more intensely when the word becomes incarnate in a deed ; so the thought of God which dwells within man burns up into passionate words in prophetic utterance, and at last finds full expression in the divine Act of the Incarnation.

And as the Incarnation is the crown and consummation of the indwelling of God in the heart of man, so it is the beginning of that mystic union in the heart of the believer by which He dwells in us and we in Him. It is related to the past and to the future. It is the first step in the crisis of that age-long process by which God works out man's redemption.

4. THE METHOD OF THE INCARNATION

The method of the Incarnation emphasizes the two marks of the Atonement which we have already noticed : Sin, in separating us from God, destroys the supernatural union between God and man, and disorders man's nature ; Atonement, reunion, must therefore be supernatural and co-operative. It must come from above ; it must work from within. It must re-create what has been destroyed in the soul of man ; and it must restore to health those natural powers of man which have become diseased and disordered. It must re-create and heal. The supernatural action of God in re-creating that union which sin had destroyed is seen in the Virgin Birth. The co-operative work of the Atonement is seen in the way in which our dear Redeemer heals and educates the powers of man's nature into healthy and harmonious activity. He does not merely impose the gift of His own nature upon us from outside, as it were ; He evokes a response to that gift from our inmost heart. He begins by purifying the springs of our life in the mother's womb. Then, by becoming dependent upon us for His own life, He educates us to love and serve Him. In this dependence He reveals to us one great secret of our redemption. It must always work from within, not merely by giving us what we have not, but by purifying and educating what we have. So He hangs a helpless infant upon His Mother's breast, in order that He may train and educate us to do our best for Him. Our diseased and disordered faculties still retain something which is not wholly bad ; and He trains this and evokes—or educates—it into healthy and harmonious activity. This co-operative side of God's redemption is a truth of experience which we can see at work in daily life. Men are not redeemed by patronage, but by sympathy. Patronage bestows upon us what we have not. Sympathy asks us for what we have. Patronage says simply " You need me." Sympathy says also " I need you." In bringing sinful souls to their Saviour it is a vital point to make great demands upon them for their best. Something good and tender and noble lingers, even in the most degraded and debased; and we must evoke this and educate it into fuller activity. Something of tenderness can be found in the most hardened heart; something of love remains in the most selfish disposition; many a mean and degraded soul will respond to the call of chivalry or heroism, if only the right note is struck.

In one of the homes of the Church Army there was a criminal whom every effort failed to reclaim. The man was subject to fearful fits of temper, and became so violent that no one could go near him. He was possessed by a devil. He would not obey any order given; and work in the garden, which often has such a wonderful power in redeeming ordinary cases, entirely failed with him. But one day the mother of the home noticed that, while he was scrubbing the kitchen floor, the eyes of the poor fellow were always wandering to the corner where her little baby lay in its cradle. She asked him whether he would kindly rock the cradle for a little; and then, by a stroke of genius, or rather by a divine inspiration, she took her little baby from the cradle and placed it in the arms of this poor devil-haunted criminal, and asked him to mind the baby while she was upstairs. For an hour he walked up and down the kitchen, tenderly cuddling the little infant to his breast, talking to it, singing to it, and waiting on its every mood with the eager service of a willing slave. To " mind the baby " soon became his daily joy ; and the awful responsibility of such a precious trust redeemed him. When after this the mother found her orders met with stubborn disobedience and saw the flame of passion kindling in the man's eyes, the brewing of the storm which used to burst with such appalling fury, she would say quietly, " If you won't do what you are told to do and can't control your temper, I shall be afraid to trust you with my baby " ; and at once the stubborn will would bend in obedience, and the storm of anger would die away from the heart in which the appeal of a helpless infant had reawakened love.

So God entrusted the Babe of Bethlehem to a lost and devil-haunted world, redeeming us not merely by the bestowal of His own life but also by the restoration of ours, calling out, educing, educating all our natural powers—by making demands upon us for ministry, healing our diseased human nature by educating our heart and mind and will into healthy and harmonious activity in His service.

It is necessary to emphasize this aspect of our redemption, for an attempt is being made to revert to the old and somewhat misleading preaching of mere substitution, and to concentrate our attention on the Cross alone as the method of the Atonement, almost to the exclusion of the Incarnation. The Cross is indeed central, but it is not exclusive. It is right to insist that, by the free action of God's mercy, " all has been done *for* us." But this formula needs to be supplemented by another : " All must be done *in* us," if we are fully to grasp the method of the Atonement. It must be co-operative as well as supernatural. It must come from above ; it must work from within. Man must be made " at one " with God by God's free creative act. He must also be made " at one " with himself by the healing of heart and mind and will

For that meaning has been much perverted by a theology which seems to have lost the proportion of the Faith by exclusive emphasis on the Death of Christ. This perversion has given to sacrifice a negative significance which does not belong to it. Sacrifice is not negative, but positive. It is not the reluctant surrender of what we want to keep, but the joyful oblation of all we have and are. Split the word up into the two parts of its derivation, and we have " sacrum facere " " to make sacred," " to consecrate," " to set apart for God." To sacrifice is not to kill, but to consecrate. Death is associated with sacrifice, primarily because of sin. The loss of life by the severance of the soul from the body is the just penalty for sin, and a symbol of that eternal death which is ours when sin finally separates the soul from God Who is its life. Death also is associated with sacrifice as the final test of the perfection and entirety of the consecration—" even unto death." Death separates a life from lower activities, so that the life sacrificed is devoted to God alone.

Again, Death enters into sacrifice as the only method of liberating life into full activity. " Except a grain of wheat fall into the earth and die, it abideth by itself alone : but if it die, it beareth much fruit " (St. John xii. 24). But while Death is associated with sacrifice as its crown and test and seal, we do not find in it the essence of sacrifice. As we have noticed above, to sacrifice is not to kill, but to consecrate. The essence of sacrifice is the entire consecration of the will in eager, loving response to the Will of God. The symbol of sacrifice is not the knife which slays, but the flame which kindles. The sacrifice of Christ was not His death, but His obedience : not His death, but His willingness to die. He became " obedient even unto death, yea, the death of the Cross " (Phil. ii. 8). The death was the test and the seal of His obedience : but what is pleasing to the Father was not the death of Christ, but His willingness to die.

Thus it is that in the life of Christ we find the essence, though not the consummation, of His sacrifice. Moment by moment, day by day, from the first movement of His human will He offered to the Father the perfect response of entire consecration :—a body unstained by sin, a mind which perfectly reflected the Father's thoughts, a heart aflame with love for the Father, a will alert, eager, concentrated in perfect response to the Father's Will. To be obedient to every movement of the Will " of Him that sent Me " was the consuming passion and the single motive of His life. It was the consecration of His boyhood :— "Wist ye not that I must be about my Father's business ? " (St. Luke ii. 49).

It was the purpose of His coming :—" I came down from Heaven not to do My own will, but the will of Him that sent Me " (St. John vi. 38).

It was His support in labour :—" My meat is to do the will of Him that sent Me, and to finish His work " (St. John iv. 34).

It was His victory in temptation :—" Father, if Thou be willing, let this cup pass from Me ; nevertheless not My will, but Thine, be done " (St. Luke xxii. 42).

It was His triumph on the Cross, to oppose to adversity and to present to the Father a will unstained by sin, unshaken in its loyalty, undimmed in the bright splendour of its self-surrender :—" Father, into Thy hands I commend My spirit " (St. Luke xxiii. 46).

Thus, having made our human nature " at one " with His divine Person in the Incarnation, He bears it through all our temptations unsullied in its purity, through all our sufferings unswerving in its loyalty, at every point making His human heart and mind and will "at one" with the heart and mind and will of the Father, offering moment by moment the perfect and all-sufficient sacrifice of an entirely consecrated life.

This is the second movement in the great process of At-one-ment.

The full appreciation of this part of the mystery of the Atonement gives its essential character to the Christian life as a life of entire consecration. What Christ did for us, He must do in us. His sacrifice is not a substitute for ours. He unites us to Himself in order that we too may offer ourselves as He offered Himself, a living sacrifice to God the Father. He identifies us with Himself, and Himself with us, by an interpenetration so powerful and intimate that it creates us anew, and yet so delicate that it does not destroy our freedom or our self-respect. In cleansing us from the guilt of sin, in re-creating what sin has destroyed, and healing what it has poisoned, He does for us what we cannot do for ourselves. But mere substitution would degrade and not develop our personality. So instead of "substitution" the Church teaches us "identification" as the keynote of our redemption—an identification which interpenetrates our personality without destroying it. Not "Christ instead of us," but "Christ in us, and for us," enfolding us in His larger personality, creating, empowering, nourishing, healing, restoring, educating. As in the sacred shrine of our mother's womb the identification and interpenetration of love first called us into being—created, nourished, strengthened us : so in the sacred shrine of the Heart of Jesus we are re-created, nourished, strengthened, healed, and restored.

CHAPTER IV

THE PASSION OF CHRIST

AS we watch the Procession in time and space winding up the mount of God, we notice that at a certain point a new dynamic begins to energize in the lives of men. Of course, when any person joins the procession there is a new force affecting the course of History. When that personality is withdrawn by death, it leaves behind it the influence of its thoughts and words and deeds which are knit into the woven pattern of human life, caught up into its mechanism, and in their degree affect the course of history. But in the case of ordinary persons it is not easy to trace anything more than the influence of their activities in time. We do not deny that they may still influence our lives. Nay, rather, we assert it. The prayers of the saints beyond the veil are energizing on our behalf. We do not know enough to dogmatize on the extent to which the departed can influence our lives.

But it is not so with the Life which was liberated into universal activity by the Sacrifice which was consummated on the Cross of Calvary. In this case history reveals a new dynamic force continuously at work in the lives of men, shattering the power of Satan, breaking the bonds of sin, liberating, re-creating, healing, restoring, redeeming innumerable souls. From the Cross of Christ we may trace this influence at work.

We do not propose to attempt an exhaustive analysis

47

of the place of the Passion in the great process of Atonement. We will only attempt to emphasize a few points which may enrich our meditation on this mystery and enable us to think of it aright.

1. THE PERSON AND WORK OF SATAN

Perhaps the first point we ought to emphasize is that we are not likely to meditate aright on this mystery if we omit one of the factors in the Passion which was most constantly present to the mind of our dear Redeemer, namely, the person and work and power of Satan. In fact, we might state this more strongly, and assert boldly that we are sure to get a distorted and inadequate view of this mystery if we omit Satan from our meditation. In giving due weight to this factor or agent in the mystery of evil which the Atonement has to meet, we need not—nay, we must not—attempt to assign him a definite place, or get entangled in those profitless discussions as to whether or not our ransom was paid to Satan. Again, we must beware of that moral feebleness, as old as human history, which too readily attributes to Satan the guilt which belongs to ourselves—" the serpent beguiled me " (Gen. iii. 13). But, moving with caution amidst mysteries of bewildering darkness and blinding light, our only wisdom is to keep as near as we can to our Guide. And our Lord in unveiling His Heart to us reveals a deep consciousness of Satan, his person and his power and his work. It is probably the neglect of this factor which makes the works of rationalist and modernist writers on the Atonement so futile, and so utterly without power to save. Modern writers on the Atonement in almost every case omit all reference to Satan, possibly because, while cherishing a superstitious reverence for the modern mind, they fear to be accused of mediæval superstition. We do not share this superstitious reverence. The modern mind may be the best we can do to-day ; but it is only the latest of innumerable modern minds, each of which has been largely discredited, and partly disowned by those which succeed it. It is the wisest course to distrust the modern mind whenever it seems out of harmony with the Mind of Christ. And yet even writers who tell us that they accept our Lord's witness as to His Person, His consciousness and mission discuss the Atonement with scarcely any reference to the person and work of Satan, although this formed so important an element in the mind of our Lord. This omission is probably due to the unscientific prejudice of a scientific age. But the truly scientific mind refuses to speculate on the spirit world. Science has nothing to do with the world of wills. It begins its work when spirits issue from the world of wills into the world of phenomena. Science begins to deal with spirits only when, and in so far as, spirit energizes in the world of phenomena. When things begin to appear, science observes and correlates them. When they cease to appear, science, strictly speaking, is no longer concerned with them. When scientific men exceed this limitation, they no longer speak as men of science. Scientific men may say that they see the world of matter interpenetrated, moved and moulded by some force which they take to be the will of man : because man belongs during his earthly life in some degree to the world of phenomena. But whether the will of man is the only agent concerned in the moulding of the world or not, the scientific man, if he is true to his principles, will not and cannot say. In so far as moral and spiritual convictions affect the course of history, they come legitimately within the sphere of science. Psychology tries to unravel the mysteries of man's mind ; but if it is loyal to its scientific principles,

E

it can only deal with the mind when it manifests itself—when the mind plays upon the piano of the brain. Whether that manifestation is always a solo or sometimes a duet, science cannot tell us, for it knows nothing of ultimates such as personality. The best psychologists assure us that they often move amidst mysteries which they cannot analyse or explain ; while some of our most eminent physicists are convinced spiritists. It is perhaps true to say that science is purely agnostic with regard to the spirit world. It neither affirms nor denies anything at all with regard to the possibility of the influence of spirits, good or evil, on man's personality. There is nothing in the psychology of our time which discredits the psychology of our Lord's time ; nor will there be, until we have come nearer to solving many a mystery, such as dual personality, and obsession, and various forms of perversion. It is possible that along the lines of fuller belief in the activity of good and evil spirits we may learn how to deal more skilfully with many forms of lunacy, and nervous diseases, and spiritual distress. It is certain that we shall learn how to enter more fully into the mystery of the Passion.

Having tried to show that this prejudice which prevents many persons from believing in the reality of Satan is not justified by reason, we may now give due weight to the convictions of spiritual men. Comparative Religion brings us a universal witness, too full to be treated here, that everywhere and always men have believed in the influence upon them, for good or evil, of discarnate persons. Space will only allow us to glance at the witness of three persons whom even the mere rationalist will recognize as pre-eminent in their claim to attention when they speak of spiritual things, viz. St. John, St. Paul, and our Lord. For the Christian of course their witness carries the weight of divine authority. And this witness will save us from missing one factor in the Passion and one aspect of our Redemption. For it is useless and misleading for us to meditate on these Mysteries as though they involved only the will of man and the Will of God, when He Who accomplished our redemption and those who first witnessed to it include in the great mystery of evil the will of Satan and the activities of evil spirits.

(i.) *In the Writings of St. Paul and St. John.*

St. Paul and St. John, who have above all revealed to us the mind of the Master, are always conscious of the presence of discarnate spirits.

St. John sees in Satan one who threatens the lives of Christians. "We know that whosoever is begotten of God sinneth not; but He that was begotten of God keepeth him, and the evil one toucheth him not. We know that we are of God, and the whole world lieth in the evil one" (1 St. John v. 18, 19). He sees the purpose of the Incarnation to be the destruction of the Devil's power. "To this end was the Son of God manifested, that He might destroy the works of the devil" (*ibid.* iii. 8). He sees that man when he sins associates himself with the evil will of the Devil. "He that doeth sin is of the devil; for the devil sinneth from the beginning" (*ibid.*). Such become "children of the devil" (*ibid.* iii. 10).

In the book of the Revelation, in vision after vision in which are revealed to us the vast spiritual forces which play upon the lives of men, behind the beast and the false prophet there is always Satan giving them life and power. And in an age like ours, so prolific of false prophets, so terribly dominated by the power of the beast, we can ill afford to ignore him who is their inspiration and their life.

And turning to St. Paul, we find a vivid consciousness that " our wrestling is not against flesh and blood, but against the principalities, against the powers, against the world-rulers of this darkness, against the spiritual hosts of wickedness in the heavenly places " (Eph. vi. 12). We were dead in trespasses and sins, walking " according to the prince of the power of the air " (*ibid.* ii. 2). On the Cross, Christ " having put off from Himself the principalities and the powers, . . . made a show of them openly, triumphing over them in it " (Col. ii. 15). Again, St. Paul is conscious that Satan hinders his work ;—" Satan hindered us " (1 Thess. ii. 18), and blinds the minds of men (see 2 Cor. iv. 4) ; he enables the lawless one to work " lying wonders " (2 Thess. ii. 9), and appears as " an angel of light " (2 Cor. xi. 14). The writer frequently exhorts believers to resist the devil ;—" And the God of peace shall bruise Satan under your feet shortly " (Rom. xvi. 20 ; see also 2 Cor. ii. 11 ; Eph. iv. 27, vi. 16 ; etc.).

It must be remembered that the early Christians lived in daily contact with idolatry and devil worship, and therefore had a more vivid realization of the activities of Satan than we have to-day in Europe, where idolatry has changed its form, and where Christianity is nominally accepted. St. Paul knew what spirit moved behind those idols :— " But I say, that the things which the Gentiles sacrifice, they sacrifice to devils, and not to God : and I would not that ye should have communion with devils. Ye cannot drink the cup of the Lord, and the cup of devils : ye cannot partake of the table of the Lord and of the table of devils " (1 Cor. x. 20, 21). In addition to these references in their letters to the powers of evil, we must bear in mind that the casting out of evil spirits was a normal part of the labour and ministry of the

Apostles (St. Mark ix. 38 ; St. Luke x. 17 ; Acts xix. 12). And in this vivid consciousness of the presence and working of the Devil, these Apostles faithfully reproduce the Mind of Christ.

(ii.) *In our Lord's Witness.*

For when we turn to our Lord's witness, we note that the account of His Temptation in the Wilderness could only have come to the knowledge of those who record it from our Lord Himself (see St. Matt. iv. 1–11 ; St. Mark i. 12, 13 ; St. Luke iv. 1–13).

His active ministry was marked by the incessant casting out of evil spirits. From the moment of His temptation forward, He is vividly conscious of a direct conflict with Satan and the spirits of evil. He commissions His Apostles to cast out evil spirits. "He called the twelve together, and gave them power and authority over all devils" (St. Luke ix. 1). "He gave them authority over unclean spirits, to cast them out" (St. Matt. x. 1 ; see also St. Mark iii. 15 ; St. Luke x. 17). He is conscious that the Devil is in the Upper Chamber testing the hearts of His Apostles :—" Simon, Simon, behold, Satan asked to have you, that he might sift you as wheat" (St. Luke xxii. 31). And as the crisis of His Passion approaches, He feels the full force of Satan's power concentrated upon Himself. "I will no more speak much with you, for the prince of this world cometh ; and he hath nothing in Me" (St. John xiv. 30). "Now is the judgment of this world : now shall the prince of this world be cast out. And I, if I be lifted up from the earth, will draw all men unto Myself" (St. John xii. 31, 32). And in parable after parable our Lord shows the devil at work hindering the coming of the Kingdom, blinding and deceiving men.

May we not say, then, that any meditation on the

mysteries of our Redemption is inadequate which entirely omits that factor in it which had so large a place in the mind of Christ ?   The teaching of St. John and the writer of the Epistle to the Hebrews is to be accepted. "To this end was the Son of God manifested, that He might destroy the works of the devil" (1 St. John iii. 8). "Since then the children are sharers in flesh and blood, He also Himself in like manner partook of the same ; that through death He might bring to nought him that had the power of death, that is, the devil" (Heb. ii. 14). We do not profess to know either the extent or the limitations of Satan's activity. We only wish to insist that when in Christ God took sin into Himself in order that He might destroy it, He shattered that awful power of Satan which paralyses the soul of man and holds it spellbound in its mesmerism. To some who have never been brought into direct contact with sin in its deeper movements this aspect of the Passion may mean little ; but to those who are sensitive to the spirit-world and know something of the mystery of evil, the shattering of Satan's power is the chief splendour of Christ's victory.

> "For Judah's Lion bursts His chains,
>   Crushing the Serpent's head ;
> And cries aloud through death's domains
>   To wake the imprison'd dead."

2. The Unity and Solidarity in the Spirit-World

The death of Christ is often spoken of as affecting the whole world, and He is described as "the Saviour of the world" (St. John i. 29, iii. 16, iv. 42 ; 1 St. John ii. 2, iv. 14 ; 2 Cor. v. 14, 15 ; Rom. v. 15). If we are to grasp this cosmic aspect of the Passion, we must first try to realize what is meant by the solidarity of the human race, and probably also of the spirit-world. We must correct in ourselves the habit of regarding each man as merely an isolated unit, closed in and shut off, and entirely independent of every other unit. Science and Philosophy, in persistently striving after unity and solidarity in Nature, have done much to shatter the " atomic " view of personality, which regarded each person as an isolated unit. We know now that in the material universe every disturbance in any part in its degree affects the whole. We know that we do not begin our conscious life on earth as separate isolated individuals, but that by heredity we are knit into the common stock of humanity, and that our freedom is qualified by vast necessities which encompass us on every side. We recognize that each person has the ultimate power of self-determination, and in this is a responsible individual. But we recognize also that the truth of our nature is incomplete as long as we think of ourselves merely as individuals. The family—that " trinity in unity " of father, mother, son—is the true unit of the human race. Our personality is essentially corporate as well as individual, and can only be fully realized as we learn to sacrifice the individual life to the life of the whole. A man can only come to the fullness of his personality as he allows himself to be merged in the larger life of family, regiment, city, nation, and race. So in the spirit-world our soul, without losing its personal responsibility, is knit into the life of all created spirits. Perhaps we can best realize this solidarity in the spirit-world by looking down from the Mount of God on a series of visions.

The first vision is one of harmony, where all wills respond to the Will of God.

The second vision is one of discord, where we see the harmony of wills rent from top to bottom by sin, beginning with the fall of the rebel angels.

The third vision is one of harmony restored by the

Atonement, wherein the Son of God makes human nature at one with Himself in order that He may make it "at one" with the Father.

The fourth vision is one of two streams of forces, one leading Godward, the other away from God. One stream is the life of Christ liberated by death, and energizing in those with whom He identifies Himself by grace and who identify themselves with Him by faith; the other is the stream of evil wills of those who by sin join themselves to Satan and his evil spirits. No spirit stands alone in absolute isolation. Every soul associates itself either with one or other stream of power, either with the obedient or with the rebellious, will into which the spirit-world is divided.

In such visions, of course, it must be carefully borne in mind that Satan is not equivalent to Christ. He is only a created spirit, not infinite, nor omnipresent, nor omniscient. He is only a leader of the rebellion,—the instigator, though not the responsible author, of our sin.

Having glanced at these visions and seen in them the eternal purpose of God to redeem, we may now see how that purpose becomes actual, that is, is realized in "acts," in the Time series.

3. THE PASSION IS TIMELESS

Before considering the Passion in its fulfilment and manifestation on the stage of History, it is well to remind ourselves that it is not only historical but also Timeless. "The Lamb" was "slain from the foundation of the world" (Rev. xiii. 8). God has always suffered when men sinned. In the crisis on the Cross of Calvary He reveals sin in its true nature and takes it upon Himself; and, by suffering the punishment and destroying the power of our sin, He is able to forgive the sinner without weakening the hostility of God's Holiness to sin. But that finished work which was completed and fulfilled on Calvary is for ever pleaded before the Father's face, and applied anew to each sinful soul. For every sin in its degree still separates the soul from God ; and every sinner still needs to be reconciled to God by the Blood of Christ. The Sacrifice is full, perfect, and sufficient ; the world is redeemed ; the power of Satan is shattered ; man is free ; the way to the Father is opened. But this Sacrifice must be continually pleaded, the Blood must be continually applied ; each individual soul must be caught up into union with that Life which reunites us to God, uplifted into the At-one-ment. Christ does not merely redeem the race. He redeems each single soul which will accept Him as its Saviour : and this redemption can only be by identification ; and this identification makes it certain that Christ is crucified afresh when we wilfully sin against Him. The Passion, then, is a present reality ; not merely a dim far-off event upon the stage of history which is being borne further and further away from us upon the receding years, but something which happens here and now. The realization of this truth will deepen our hatred of sin and quicken our love for our Saviour.

4. THE PASSION, A PRESENT REALITY

Once a schoolboy, as he knelt by the side of his mother in her silent watch in church, saw the tears flowing freely from her eyes and asked her, " Mother, why are you crying ? " The mother answered, " Because our sins have crucified our Saviour." When, later on, at school this boy knelt before his crucifix at nights to say his evening prayers, he used to puzzle over his mother's saying. He would say to himself, " How can my sins crucify my Saviour ? He was crucified so long ago

—nearly two thousand years. I wish I could have been there by His side, and, if I had had the courage, I would have stuck up for Him, and not deserted Him. But that was all so long ago!" Then he would argue with himself: "If someone who loves me very much and whom I love—my mother, for instance—were hanging on the cross to-day, and every time I sinned someone smote her in the face, or stabbed her with a knife, how I should hate my sins then!" Then God revealed to him that this is what really does happen, that Jesus is a living present Saviour Who loves him as He loved Peter and John in the days of old, loves him more even than his mother could love him, Who here and now is disappointed when we fail to love and serve Him, Who suffers when we sin. So the Passion became to that boy a present reality; and Jesus was known to him no longer as a far-off dim figure who moved once across the stage of history, but as a living, loving, present Saviour Whose life is knit with his. His religion was transfigured from a dead form into a living communion: and the boy, when he made his confessions, knew now what his sins cost the Heart of Jesus. And is not this revelation justified by a true and living theology of the living Christ? If we can say that "God is love," are we not also forced to say that God must suffer when we sin? Is such a thing possible as a love which is indifferent to a response? What love would that be which was indifferent as to whether the loved one returned its love or not, or which could look on unmoved while sin ate away the power of loving from the soul which it loved? Plainly, to say that God is love is to say that God suffers when we sin. And when we turn to our Bibles is not this fundamental truth of the philosophy of love justified there? Do we not read that those who sin wilfully "crucify to themselves the Son of God

afresh, and put Him to an open shame " ? (Heb. vi. 6).
Is the Heart of Jesus changed, or is He still the same as
in the days of old ? " Jesus Christ the same yesterday,
to-day, and for ever " (Heb. xiii. 8). When eight years
after His Ascension He met Saul on the road to Damascus,
did He say, " Saul, Saul, why persecutest thou My followers ? " Did He not say, " Why persecutest thou
Me ? " And in that word we realize the living truth of
the Gospel of Identification, that Christ saves us by
making each one of us " at one " with Him, that He may
dwell in us and we in Him. Will not the King say at
the last day, " Inasmuch as ye did it unto one of these
My brethren, even these least, ye did it unto Me " ; and is
not this the perpetual sanction and inspiration of all social
work ? (St. Matt. xxv. 40). Without questioning then
the perfection of that finished work on Calvary, and its
finality and all-sufficiency in our redemption, we may
realize that each incident of the Passion is not merely a
fact—a thing done—in history, but is also the manifestation in time of an age-long state. There are passages
in the Epistle to the Hebrews which so emphasize the
finality of Christ's work for us that they seem to conflict
with the certainty that Christ still suffers when we sin.
We cannot tell how the author of that Epistle would
reconcile such passages with those others which teach
us that He still suffers (Heb. vi. 6, x. 29, xiii. 8) ; but we
know that any interpretation must be false which conflicts
with the certainty that if Christ still loves us He must
still suffer when we sin.

5. Concurrent Processes

Perhaps the solution of this difficulty is to be found in
the idea of concurrent processes—that each event in the
life of Christ on earth is the manifestation in Time of a

process which is always going on in the life of our dear Redeemer as He lives it out in the hearts of the redeemed. The Incarnation is a fact in History. It is also a continuous process by which in every Baptism and in every Eucharist Christ unites Himself with the body and soul of each one whom He incorporates into His divine Humanity. The Passion is a fact in History. It is also a continuous process by which Christ always suffers when we sin. The Resurrection, too, is a fact in History. It is also a continuous process by which in our repentance we are caught up into "the power of the Resurrection." "If ye then be risen with Christ . . ." (Col. iii. 1). The Ascension, also, is a fact in History. But it is also a continuous process by which, when we aspire after holiness, we are caught up to move in heavenly places with Him so that "in heart and mind we may thither ascend, and with Him continually dwell."

We may now enter more fully into the true power and meaning of the Passion.

CHAPTER V

THE DEATH OF CHRIST

IN meditating on the Passion of our dear Redeemer, we remind ourselves that we can only know a little of its real bitterness. For sin has blunted our spiritual perception: our hearts can never be as sensitive as His. So we will remember that we are watching the suffering of the One Who is " holy, harmless, undefiled, separate from sinners " (Heb. vii. 26).

1. The Friend of Sinners

Human analogy will help us to form some faint idea of what contact with sin must have meant to Him. We know how we love and reverence the pure and radiant innocence of a little child, and how the evil word is hushed and the evil deed is hidden in its presence. We know how the pure heart of a good girl suffers when she first becomes aware of sin. So we can faintly picture to ourselves what the Heart of Jesus must have suffered when He identified Himself with sinners. Yet we must bear in mind that, though He became responsible for our sins, they found no place in Him, no answer to their appeal in His Heart. We must remember also that He, in the purity of His sinless nature, felt sin more deeply than we can ever do, because He knew, as we cannot know, the Holiness of God. Men generally think of sin in its social bearing or in its destructive effect on man's nature: Christ always sees it first as an offence against God's Holiness. Moving, as He did habitually move, in the full and conscious light of the open heavens and the vision of the Father's face, sin was always most loathsome to Him as a transgression of the Law of Holiness and Righteousness and Love which *is* God's nature,—not a fiat of God's Will, but His very Being.   In the Heart of Jesus the full reaction of God's Holiness against sin, the full judgment and condemnation of God upon sin was always present. And yet it was His mission, "the Will of Him that sent Me," not only to associate with sinners, but to accept the full responsibility for their sin as though it were His own, to be so associated with our sins that they clung around Him though they found no entrance into Him.

2. A Voluntary Death

Reverence makes us shrink from discussions as to when He realized that it was His mission to become a curse for us, to bear the penalty as well as the reproach of our sins, to be the Victim in order that He might become our Great High Priest.   But, though we cannot tell when He first realized it, we know when He first revealed it to His Apostles.   Throughout His ministry He associated Himself with conscious sinners, avoiding the society of the self-righteous.   He was "a friend of publicans and sinners" (St. Matt. ix. 10–13, xi. 19, xxi. 31; St. Mark ii. 15–17; St. Luke v. 29–32, vii. 34).   He felt that His mission was to save the lost (St. Matt. x. 6, xv. 24; St. Luke xv. 4, xix. 10).   But of the death which His mission involved He first spoke just before the moment of His highest exaltation on the Mount of Transfiguration.   "From that time began Jesus to shew unto His disciples, how that He must go unto Jerusalem, and suffer many things of the elders and chief priests and scribes, and be killed, and the third day be raised up" (St. Matt. xvi. 21).   At the Transfiguration He spake with Moses and Elias of "His decease which He was about to accomplish at Jerusalem" (St. Luke ix. 31). And, with the Father's approval strong upon Him, He gave the Apostles a hint of His coming Passion as He bade them "tell the vision to no man, until the Son of Man be risen from the dead" (St. Matt. xvii. 9). He looked eagerly forward to the consummation of His sacrifice by death, and rebuked any attempt to divert Him from His purpose (St. Mark viii. 33). But for our consolation when we shrink from our cross, we may note that, while His purpose never faltered, His human will knew that shrinking which all brave men feel as they march to a voluntary death. "Now is my soul troubled; and what shall I say? Father, save me from this hour. But for this cause came I unto this hour. Father, glorify Thy Name" (St. John xii. 27, 28). It was this fixed purpose to die for us which made Him eagerly desire to institute the Holy Eucharist as the first action of His Passion. "With desire I have desired to eat this passover with you before I suffer" (St. Luke xxii. 15); or, as we may interpret it, "Earnestly have I longed to eat this passover with you before I suffer: for I tell you that I certainly shall not eat one again till its full meaning has been brought out in the Kingdom of God."[1] His was a voluntary death. He might have avoided it. "Therefore doth my Father love Me, because I lay down My life, that I may take it again. No one taketh it away from Me, but I lay it down of Myself" (St. John x. 17, 18).

So the last Passover is celebrated; and what till then had been only a memory and a hope, is now fulfilled, as the Lamb of God consecrates the Bread to be His Body, and the Wine to be His Blood—"Himself the Victim, and Himself the Priest."

[1] See Weymouth, *The New Testament in Modern Speech*.

3. GETHSEMANE

In Gethsemane we find the crisis of the Passion, and watch with deepest awe and reverence the working out of a further phase in the process of the Atonement. For it is there that we see our Lord making His Human Will " at one " with the Will of the Father. We cannot expect to know the inner reality of that agony in the Garden where we see

> " Desperate tides of the whole great world's anguish
> Forced through the channels of a single heart."

But, as He asked the three Apostles for the support of their sympathy when He was passing through that awful agony, we too may meditate upon that hour when He could say, " My soul is exceeding sorrowful, even unto death " (St. Matt. xxvi. 38). We know how sensitive the sacred Heart was to the sorrows of the world, how richly and how deeply He had loved, how His Heart went out in deep divine compassion to the leper, the outcast, the mourner, and the multitude. In Him had been fully realized that only exhaustive definition of Life—" To live is to love. To love is the perfect tense of the verb to live." But love is not love unless it yearns for a response, unless it rejoices to be met by an answering love however feeble, and bleeds when no answer comes. So the Heart of Jesus bleeds when the world which He loves does not want Him. And here let us pause to insist on one point to which allusion has already been made, viz. that the Passion is timeless, that though it is of necessity wrought out on the stage of history, its inner reality is the same to-day as when He first bore it. The Heart of Jesus does not change. " Jesus Christ is the same yesterday, and to-day, yea and for ever " (Heb. xiii. 8). We know how easy it is to serve God in prosperity and how hard it is to retain our courage in adversity. When the mother who has spent a lifetime of love upon her son and has lived only in and for him, awakens to realize that he is so fully absorbed in his own schemes and ambitions that his heart is dead towards her and that she is not wanted, she knows something of what our Saviour felt in that awful agony in the Garden.

But while no merely human experience will give us an exact analogy—for our consciousness is not as large as His—yet, if we examine many cases which are familiar to our experience, without pressing the details of any particular case, we may get a dim and blurred impression of what He must have suffered. And a dim impression is all that is possible for us whose conscience and heart have lost something of their sensitiveness because they have been stained or blunted or hardened by sin.

If we examine cases of corporate responsibility as contrasted with merely individual responsibility, we may vaguely understand something of the burden of the sins of the whole world which lay on His Heart. And if we examine many aspects of death, we may dimly conceive what it was which so troubled His soul as He set His face like a flint in Gethsemane to meet the death upon the Cross of Calvary. Only let us remind ourselves again that no single case will afford an exact analogy in detail. The value of this method depends on the progressive accumulation of vague impressions which make up a total—indefinite, imperfect, but real and true as far as we sinful creatures can realize the sufferings of our sinless Creator and Redeemer.

4. Cases of Corporate Responsibility

First, let us take corporate responsibility. We have seen that the atomic theory of personality which treats

F

each person as a separated, isolated, solitary individual is absolutely untrue to experience, and is condemned as false by Science and Philosophy. Personality is fundamentally and essentially social ; and the individual can only find himself as he loses himself in a larger life. The wider the range of his love becomes, and the more perfect his self-abandonment, the richer will be his experiences and the larger the range of his personality : utter self-abandonment to God means perfect self-realization : it is an immutable law of eternal life that self-sacrifice is the only way to self-realization.

Let us begin with natural unions.

(i.) *The Family*.

The husband and wife become one flesh, and share responsibility for one another in the inter-communion of a common life of soul and body.

When that union is consummated, and has become incarnate in the birth of a child, new relationships are constituted in this "trinity in unity" which has now become Father, Mother, Son. Thus God at the Incarnation knit Himself into most intimate fellowship with the human race.

This union, while it is constituted by nature, is intensified by grace. The sin of the son brings disgrace on the family. His mother's heart bleeds, his father feels the shame, though not the guilt, of his sin. This natural impulse is, for those who believe in God, intensified and deepened by supernatural sanctions. If this corporate responsibility for one another is not felt by members of a family, it means that family life is disintegrating in selfishness. It is this sense of corporate life, embracing as it does not only the present but also the past and the future, which provides the greater part of those subtle inhibitions and motives which discipline and regulate the life of a gentleman, and constitute the well-known sanction, as indefinable as it is imperative, "noblesse oblige."

(ii.) *The Nation.*

From the Family we pass on in ever-widening circles to the Tribe and the Nation and the Empire; and so to that which is to become the universal Empire, the Holy Catholic Church. In each case, the health and vitality of the corporate life is dependent on the intensity with which each single member feels responsibility for the whole; and the health of the individual life is dependent on its sensitiveness to the call which the corporate life makes upon him. The world-wide war has shown us that this solidarity of men in their national life is so fundamental and profound that no surface movements of the fretful intellect in the least affect it. Within a few hours from the time when the heart of the nation moved at the trumpet's call, the wild hatred of the cosmopolitan revolutionary for his nation had entirely evaporated, and he was marching off joyfully to die for his country. Behind all divisions of party politics, beneath all prejudices of class hatred, deeper than all cleavages in our surface life, we suddenly came upon a unity which in times of excessive and perilous prosperity had been forgotten—the instinct of patriotism, the love of our country. And by patriotism we do not mean that blind and brutal corporate self-assertion which can glory in its moral degradation—" My country, right or wrong," but that flame which burns in the heart and on the lips of every prophet who can rebuke his nation's sins, and weep for her shame, and die for her honour.

(iii.) *The Race.*

And as war has revealed the deep fundamental instinct of the corporate life in nationality, may we not hope

that Peace will reveal a still wider unity wherein, purged
from their sins, the nations may realize their brotherhood
in the bond of Human Nature ?   But this racial unity
to which we are moving can never be realized by sinful
men who merely wish to escape the penalty of their
sins.   Not by sentimental aspirations, but only by a
world-wide repentance can those sins which separate
nations from one another be removed.   As long as our
social and economic life is based on the selfishness of
unrestrained competition, it is based on sin : and until
co-operation, instead of unrestrained competition, is
made the basal principle of human intercourse, we cannot
escape our doom.   The life which is based on selfishness is
based on sin : and the wages of sin is death.   Unless the
selfish heart of man is changed, the nations must march
again, through years of peace, to the inevitable doom of a
universal war of mutual extermination.   Can anyone
save us from this inevitable doom ?   Only one—" the
Lamb of God Which taketh away the sins of the world."

(iv.) *The Messiah.*

As the family finds its corporate life summed up in
the Father ; as the nation gathers up its corporate life
in King or Ruler ; so the race is summed up into
personal unity in the Person of the Son of God, Who
became the Son of Man in order that the sons of men
might become the sons of God.   He is the Christ, the
Servant of the Lord, the Anointed One, the Messiah, the
King, the Priest of the Human Race.   In Him all Humanity
finds personal expression, and becomes capable of corporate
action, of corporate repentance and return to God.   As the
father bears the responsibility and the penalty and shame,
but not the guilt, of the sins of the family, so the Christ
must bear the burden of the sins of the whole world.

It was this realization of His mission as the Messiah which filled our Lord's mind throughout His ministry ; and He realized that of divine necessity, and not merely of human malice, it involved a shameful death, if sin was to be conquered and the power of Satan shattered, and death robbed of its sting, and the race redeemed.

Having considered the nature of corporate life and the solidarity of the Human Race, and seen it summed up in the Christ, we may now pass on to meditate on the moral character of death. For death is as varied as life itself in its character.

5. CASES OF DEATH

(i.) *An Event.*

We first look at death as an event. It is the universal and inevitable close of every human life. It is the separation of the soul from the body, the dissolution of a partnership which has been so intimate in its inter-penetration that the body cannot survive the separation. It is the end of human opportunity, the seal of one phase of a life. It is a transition from the known and familiar to the unknown and strange, and therefore it must be full of awe.

It is the sealing up of normal intercourse with certain friends whom one leaves behind. It is a great adventure.

So far, the event in itself. Now let us note some of the circumstances which affect the character of a death.

(ii.) *Accidental Death.*

Death may be merely the normal closing on earth of a life which has run its course, as when the aged die. Or it may be due to sickness or to accident. These may come upon us as the result of our own or of another's sin—as in the case of inherited disease or murder : and thus may be clothed with varying degrees of pathos.

In these cases death is an incident which chiefly affects the individual.

(iii.) *Sacrificial Death.*

Death may be sacrificial, when a man dies for others. And this may be either incidental or deliberate: incidental, as when a doctor dies from a disease caught in his efforts to save the life of his patient : deliberate, as when a man chooses to die in order that a friend may live. Thus in the ice-bound regions of the South Pole where Death reigns supreme, a solitary cross speaks to the silent stars of a sacrificial death, where it marks the grave of Captain Oates, who to save his comrades' lives faced the blizzard, and marched steadily through the gates of death to the life beyond, quickening the heart of the world into a flame of gratitude.

Thus every Victoria Cross which adorns the breast of a hero is only a symbol which glows with the splendour of a thousand unrecorded deeds of heroism. For each one who wins the Victoria Cross there are a thousand deeds of heroism, unseen by any eye but the eye of God, as day and night in the trenches men die in trying to save a comrade's life.

A mother may choose to die in order that her child may live. These two notes—" on behalf of others " and "of one's own free will "—conform such deaths in their degree to the Death of Christ.

(iv.) *Death for a Cause.*

But we may add to the range of sacrifice a wider circle than that merely of family or friendship. A man may die for a cause or a people. The prophet to whom God has entrusted a word of righteousness and justice may die broken-hearted amidst the persecutions of those whose vested interests he has imperilled by his preaching.

He becomes a martyr to a cause, and dies for the people. A priest may deliberately choose to forsake the pleasant things of life, and to lose health and strength and life itself in ministering to the poor in some unhealthy slum. These are still closer to the sacrifice of Christ.

(v.) *A Soldier's Death.*

A soldier's death, in a war as holy as this to which God has called us, is united to the death of Christ and helps us to realize His Sacrifice, because it bears these three marks upon it. First, Obedience. The soldier does not die seeking his own pleasure or gain, or following his own will. He suffers and dies because he is obedient to a command from a superior will. And obedience is the very essence of sacrifice. Secondly, he dies of his own free will. He might have refused the call of God, and stayed at home in a shameful security. But now that the nature of this war is clear and men know what they have to face, the mystic glow of sacrifice burns in the heart and kindles in the eyes of many a lad as he marches off to face suffering and death in order that a Righteous Will may prevail. Men will never understand what it is in a soldier's life which attracts and exalts, until they realize that killing is only incidental to a soldier's profession. It is not the aim. The aim is to make a Righteous Will prevail, and this at any cost, even of the man's own death or the death of his enemy. That which exalts it on to the level of sacrifice is that the soldier faces suffering and death for great spiritual issues, and proclaims to all the world that he loves liberty more than life, and fears dishonour more than death.

Again, a soldier's death is closely united to the Sacrifice of Christ because he does not die for himself but for others. As we weep for our slain, we remember that through their death generations yet unborn will live in Peace and Liberty, because, when God called, in our own land alone, three millions of our lads answered to the call, and offered their lives as a sacrifice on our behalf.

We follow Charles Gordon through his life of utter self-sacrifice. We watch him at his prayers. We see his face glow with the light of another world, as the Angels of God meet him when he marches forth to battle; and those will surely judge amiss who think only of the men he slew, and forget the millions he liberated over vast regions of the earth by the glad surrender of his life.

But, because the soldier of necessity uses force in the fulfilment of his mission, we must look higher still to find a loftier approach to the death of Christ.

(vi.) *A Martyr's Death.*

In the Missionary-martyr we find one who forsakes all that the world loves, and goes forth unarmed to give his life a ransom for many. He opposes to the violence of the enemy an unconquerable meekness. He bears Truth on his lips and Love in his heart; and he opposes to Tyranny a will which knows not how to yield. Refusing to disown that Truth or to betray that Love, seeking only the salvation of those who are opposed to him, he dies the death which approaches nearest to the death of the Cross.

But there is still a distinction which marks off the death of a martyr from the death of the Messiah. For a martyr's death is only incidental to his witness. His witness is the aim of his life, and his death is only the seal on a faithful witness. He does not seek death: he merely submits to it. It was not so with the death of Christ.

6. The Messiah's Death

Christ is more than the King of Martyrs. His death is more than the inevitable consequence of His faithful witness. We cannot expect fully to understand the mysteries of divine necessities, we poor half-blinded creatures who cannot really tell why anything is what it is and not otherwise. All we can do is to note how our dear Lord looked upon His own death ; and we note that He accepted it eagerly as a preordained and essential part of His office as Messiah. It was not a penalty which could not be avoided ; it was a battle to be fought and a victory to be won. The martyr accepts death ; the Messiah seeks it. The death of the Christ is not merely due to the malice of men ; it is preordained in the eternal counsels of God. Hidden in the unfathomable depths of the mystery of evil there is a divine necessity that the Messiah, as the head of the sinful human race, shall die in order "that through death He might bring to nought him that had the power of death, that is, the devil" (Heb. ii. 14). Sin, deep-seated in the soul of man, does not lose its power when the soul is parted from the body : it penetrates beyond death into the sphere of the eternal. So the Messiah Who is to redeem us from sin must conquer death, not merely submit to it. He Who is to be the High Priest of Humanity must first become the Victim. He Who is "to bring Life and immortality to light" must shatter death by embracing it and by rising from the dead, so that the kingdom which He came to found may not be "of this world," a matter of time and space, but may be founded in the eternal sphere. It is a Kingdom of spiritual and eternal values, of Love and Holiness, of Truth and Righteousness : and as sin must not stain or bind these, so death must not limit or confine them. As by the conquest of sin death must be robbed of its sting, so by the conquest of death the grave must be robbed of its victory.

This conviction that He must meet and conquer death

in order to found the Kingdom of the Redeemed we find deep-seated in the consciousness of our dear Lord, and repeated again and again in His teaching. For Him to die was not the unfortunate and premature close of an active ministry which had excited the hostilities of powerful enemies too strong to be resisted. To meet and, by dying, to conquer, Death was to Him a predestined duty of the Messiah—a part of His office, a work to be accomplished, not a misfortune to be endured ; not a punishment to be borne, but a Will to be done.

So, in strongest contrast to the vague, anæmic, sentimental Gospel of modern literary unbelief, which wants to discard miracles and to centralize the work of Christ on His ethical teaching in the Sermon on the Mount, the Church preserves for us in her Gospel a strong, virile Christ Who burns with an eager desire to conquer sin, Satan, and death by grappling with them and breaking their power, in order that He may set man free. This is the central point of all His teaching. He has come to suffer, and to die, and to rise again. This is proclaimed as the work of the Son of Man, the Messiah, the Christ. When Peter had acknowledged Him as the Christ the Messiah, our Lord at once " began to teach them that the Son of Man must suffer many things, and be rejected by the elders, and the chief priests, and the scribes, and be killed, and after three days rise again " (St. Mark viii. 31). The Apostles could not bear this teaching, for they hoped for a conquering, not a suffering, Messiah. And our Lord meets Peter's remonstrance with the strong rebuke, "Get thee behind me, Satan, for thou mindest not the things of God, but the things of men " (*ibid.* 33). Again and again He insists on this truth, not merely in direct statement (St. Mark viii. 31, ix. 31, x. 32–34 ; St. Matt. xvi. 21 ; St. Luke ix. 22), but also in metaphor and parable. The "Bridegroom" must be "taken away from them" (St. Mark ii. 19, 20). "As Jonah was three days and three nights in the belly of the whale ; so shall the Son of Man be three days and three nights in the heart of the earth" (St. Matt. xii. 40). "The Lamb of God" (St. John i. 29) is for sacrifice. The "Temple" (*ibid*. ii. 19) will be destroyed and rebuilt. The Son of Man will be lifted up from the earth to draw all men unto Him (*ibid*. iii. 14, 15, viii. 28, xii. 32). "I will give . . . My flesh for the life of the World" (*ibid*. vi. 51). "The Good Shepherd layeth down His life for the sheep" (*ibid*. x. 11). The corn of wheat must die in order that it may bear fruit (*ibid*. xii. 24). The wicked husbandmen will slay the King's son (St. Mark xii. 6–8). Thus we may see that to die and to rise again was the work which He came to do, His mission the consuming passion of His Heart.

In meditating on the spiritual aspects of many examples of death, we reached its highest form when we thought of the death of the martyr. We noted that the martyr's death was incidental to his witness. In entering on Gethsemane to gaze with veiled faces on the agony of our dear Redeemer, we must add to every other thought of Death three considerations ;—the world-wide range of the issues, the desertion, and the shame of the death of a criminal.

When Edith Cavell, after nursing German soldiers back to life, was shot by the sentence of German officers, a thrill of horror shook the heart of the world which sobbed for the sorrows of a single heart. In Gethsemane a single Heart bore all the sins and sorrows of the whole wide world.

> " Desperate tides of the whole great world's anguish
> Forced through the channels of a single heart."

As on the Mount of Temptation He gazed undazzled on all the kingdoms of the world and the glory of them ; so on the Mount of Olives the vision returns, all the kingdoms of the world, and their sins and sorrows. "He was in the world, and the world was made by Him, and the world knew Him not" (St. John i. 10). Far into the future His eye penetrates to the utmost limits of the ages, and back to the dawn of time and man's primæval sin. Every desire of lust and every deed of shame, every flame of passion, every cold cruelty of selfishness in the vast mystery of evil clings around Him as though it were His own. Every falsehood and every act of treachery is gathered up to a point in the kiss of Judas ; every pang of love betrayed bleeds in the Sacred Heart. But far more awful even than the sins and sorrows of the world must have been that which He encountered in the central heart of the mystery of evil—the wrestling with Satan. The passionate striving among men in every age against temptation, so pathetic, so ineffectual, of those who have fallen beneath his spell, the agonies of a dying hope as the will slowly ceases to resist the mesmerism, the cold chill hand of despair as it freezes up the fountains of life—all these must have been known to the Saviour as He wrestled with Satan, and with bloody sweat slowly disentangled the will of man from the snares of the Evil One.

What mental anguish, too, He must have endured in the universal rejection ! From the time that He had taught that the Messiah must suffer, not only had the fickle multitude forsaken Him, but even His disciples did not believe in Him (*ibid*. vi. 66, vii. 5). This claim of a Galilean carpenter that He would sit on the throne of glory, and that all nations would be summoned up before Him, seemed to many the dream of a madman. "He hath a devil and is mad ; why hear ye Him ? " (*ibid*. x.

20). His friends said, "He is beside Himself" (St. Mark iii. 21). Almost the most acute agony which man can suffer is endured when on the borderland between reason and insanity, the doubts of his friends help to shake a man's belief in himself and in his own sanity. But the man knows an anguish deeper still, when a false accusation against which he cannot defend himself without a breach of trust, robs him of his character, and exposes him as a criminal to the derision of his enemies, and, still worse, to the sorrowful pity and disappointment of his friends. And when such unjust reproach falls on a priest, or someone else highly exalted in the people's trust and affections, then he may know, so far as the heart of man can ever know, something of what the Son of God suffered in Gethsemane, when He Who had proclaimed Himself as the Messiah had to face death upon the Cross as a criminal and blasphemer, cursed of God. And all this had to be sustained by the courage of His human will which must be brought through trembling and shrinking into perfect harmony with the Father's Will. This is the crisis of the Atonement, to make the will of Man " at-one " with the Will of God ; and now, having won the victory and set His face as a flint, He stands before the judgment seat of the highest spiritual court on earth and proclaims Himself the Messiah. The High Priest asked, "Art Thou the Christ, the Son of the Blessed ? " And Jesus said, "I am; and ye shall see the Son of Man sitting at the right hand of power, and coming with the clouds of heaven " (*ibid*. xiv. 61, 62).

But we must not attempt to follow our Lord through all the details of His Passion. And yet, to know what our sin costs the Heart of God, we must listen to the cry of a broken heart. "My God, my God, why hast Thou forsaken Me ? " He Who had lived His life in uninterrupted communion with the Father and in the full enjoyment of the Heavenly Vision, now finds that Vision blotted out, as the cloud of the sins of the world hides from Him the Father's Face. What must His heart have suffered! The desertion of His Apostles would not leave Him alone, for He would still have the open vision of the Father's Face. "Behold, the hour cometh, yea, is come, that ye shall be scattered every man to his own, and shall leave Me alone : and yet I am not alone, because the Father is with Me" (St. John xvi. 32). But now the sins of the world roll between Him and the Father's Face, and He tastes death for us—that separation from conscious union with the Father which is the most bitter penalty of sin.

The Heart breaks, for it can bear no more. Sorrow, sin, and Satan can break that Sacred Heart; but they cannot bend that consecrated Will which still holds on with unwavering trust and raises with a loud voice the cry of victory, "It is finished. Father, into Thy Hands I commend My Spirit." The Sacrifice is full, perfect, and sufficient for the sins of the whole world. Our sins have been taken into the Heart of God, and cleansed of their guilt. The separation between man and God is healed ; the At-one-ment has been accomplished ; the world is redeemed ; Satan's power is broken ; man is set free ; the Kingdom of Heaven is opened—through that broken Heart we have free access to the Father. Death cannot hold that Humanity which sin could not defile ; and He rises victorious from the grave, our Great High Priest, to bear the sacrifice of a sinless Human nature up through the choirs of angels to enthrone it in the Heart of God.

We have now to follow that final act of the Atonement in which our Great High Priest bears up His perfect sacrifice to present it to the Father, and through it makes us " at one " with God.

CHAPTER VI

THE LIVING CHRIST

SO far we have followed, through three of its stages, the great process of Atonement by which God makes man "at one" with Himself. We have seen that in the Incarnation the Son of God took human nature into union with His Divine Person, making it at one with Himself. Then, as we followed the footsteps of His earthly life, we saw our Lord uniting His human nature to God the Father, as day by day He offers Him the eager response of body and soul, of heart and mind and will, the sacrifice of an entirely consecrated life. Then we have seen that Sacrifice tested, sealed, and slain on Calvary when God took sin upon Himself, and bore its shame and broke its power, and by rising from the dead shattered the power of Satan, and set man free.

1. THE LAMB OF GOD

We have now to follow our dear Redeemer no longer as our Victim, but as our Great High Priest passing through the Heaven to present His Sacrifice to the Father, and to enthrone our manhood, purified from sin, in its home in the Heart of God. This glorious process of Atonement is enshrined in the whole of the covenanted worship of God, from the day when the first little lamb was slain at the temple door to the present time, when, day after day, from ten thousand altars amidst every nation, kindred, tongue, and people we hear the ceaseless adoration of the Lamb.

If we follow the Jewish ritual carefully, we find the whole process of the Atonement enshrined in sacred drama. The lamb is predestined for the Altar; it is examined to see that it is free from spot or blemish; it is sealed on the forehead with a little lump of clay bearing the Temple Seal. Then the worshipper who has purchased it brings it to the temple door, lays his hands on the head, and, pressing hard, confesses his sins; then the lamb is slain. Then the Priest, catching up the blood, which is the liberated life, in a silver bowl, bears it in solemn procession to the Altar, and sprinkles it upon the Altar and the Mercy Seat. Then he returns to join with the worshipper in communion with God as they partake of the flesh of the lamb.

So we have seen our Lord, the Lamb of God, predestined for this sacrifice, "slain from the foundations of the world," bought for thirty pieces of silver, examined by Pilate and found free from spot or blemish, the hands of sinful men pressed on Him, and, bearing all the sins of the world upon His Heart, slain on Calvary. But this is only the central point, the crisis of the drama of Atonement. We must see Him now bearing His own Blood, His sinless Humanity, His liberated Life, up through the starlit temple of the Universe, passing through the choirs of Angels and presenting His Sacrifice to the Father: and then, in the power of the Spirit, coming to be with us in the abiding communion of His Church.

2. THE ASCENSION

This was the central point of the Apostles' preaching. God had raised up and exalted the One Who had died. " This Jesus did God raise up, whereof we all are witnesses. Being therefore by the right hand of God exalted, and having received of the Father the promise of the Holy

Ghost, He hath poured forth this which ye see and hear"
(Acts ii. 32, 33). Jesus Christ "is on the right hand of
God, having gone into heaven" (1 St. Peter iii. 22). "It
is Christ Jesus that died, yea, rather that was raised from
the dead, Who is at the right hand of God. God raised
Him from the dead, and made Him to sit at His right
hand in the heavenly places. He that descended is the
same also that ascended far above all the heavens. God
highly exalted Him. He was received up in glory"
(Rom. viii. 34 ; Eph. i. 20, iv. 10 ; Phil. ii. 9 ; 1 St. Tim.
iii. 16). And in the Epistle to the Hebrews we have a
glorious picture of our great High Priest "Who hath passed
through the heavens. We have such a high priest Who
sat down on the right hand of the throne of the Majesty
in the heavens. He entered in once for all into the holy
place . . . into heaven itself, now to appear before the face
of God for us. He sat down on the right hand of God"
(Heb. iv. 14, viii. 1, ix. 12, 24, x. 12, xii. 2, as combined
by Prof. Swete in his book, *The Ascended Christ*, page 4).

It is in the Ascension and the continued activities of
our great High Priest Who "ever liveth to make intercession for" us (Heb. vii. 25), that we find the crowning
action of the process of the Atonement. In the Incarnation the Son of God embraced our human nature, and made
it "at one" with His divine Person. In the Temptation,
throughout His earthly life and in Gethsemane He disentangled our human will from the enticements of the world,
the flesh, and the Devil, and made it "at one" with the
Father's Will. On the Cross He conquered sin and Satan,
and His Sacrifice was sealed by Death. Then, since
death could not hold His sinless humanity, He uplifted
it from the grave, and bore it up triumphant to enthrone
it in the Heart of God ; and in that glorious Ascension
Man is made "at one" with God, and the Atonement is

G

accomplished, the race is redeemed. At every point it is our full humanity, body, soul, and spirit, which He reunites to God. The Atonement is not a merely spiritual movement; it is essentially sacramental. He did not leave His Body in the grave. He bore up to heaven something which He did not bring down—our Human Nature. It is into that sinless Humanity that we are baptized. It is that exalted Human Nature which He bestows on us in the Blessed Sacrament of His Body and Blood, in order that He may abide in us and we in Him. But not only is this full process of the Atonement revealed to us in Jewish ritual and Apostolic preaching; it is preserved to us in the whole prayer-life of the Holy Catholic Church. In the daily recitation of the Apostles' and Nicene Creed, in the whole action of the Holy Eucharist, and in the Fasts and Festivals of the Church's Year, the whole process of the Atonement—the Incarnation, Cross, Resurrection and Ascension—are perpetually brought before Catholic Churchmen. And the fact that these are enshrined in the prayer-life and liturgy of the Church saves us from being at the mercy of any individual preacher whose own temperament or spiritual experience might lead him to lose the proportion of the Faith by preaching too often on that aspect of the Atonement which appeals most forcibly to him. Whatever may be his particular enthusiasms, the rights of the congregation to the fullness of the Gospel are preserved; for his teaching must follow the course of the Church's Year, in which the whole process of the Atonement is preserved.

3. The Cross Central, but not Exclusive

It has been urged with much truth that the preaching of the Cross is the most powerful message for the conversion of souls. This is true; but it is only a part of the truth. Souls need much more than conversion. They need edification, building up in the Faith. Probably nothing so utterly hardens souls in spiritual pride when they themselves have been converted as listening, Sunday after Sunday, to incessant appeals to the unconverted. Nothing seems more likely to impoverish the spiritual life, or to arrest all growth in holiness, than the preaching of the Cross to the exclusion of the Incarnation, Resurrection, and Ascension. And when we look with shame and sorrow on the divisions of Christendom, may we not ask whether they are not largely due to this loss of proportion in the preaching of the Gospel? One action of God—the death upon the Cross ; one activity of man —the faith by which he surrenders himself to the Crucified—are preached almost to the exclusion of the rest, with results of great impoverishment in the spiritual life.

4. SALVATION, PRIMARILY CORPORATE

As we pass on to note how the great Atonement which has been accomplished is made available for individual souls by the outpouring of the Holy Spirit on the Church, we note that one heresy lies behind all the divisions of Christendom in our land—the heresy of Individualism. The average Protestant treats the salvation of his soul as a purely personal affair which concerns him alone. He repudiates the sacred ministry of the Church with that iniquitous saying : " I won't have anyone between my soul and God," a saying which fully embodies the Creed of Selfishness. He ignores the history and the traditions of the Church by that other saying which has become the motto of Protestantism, " The Bible, and the Bible only, is the religion of Protestants,"—a foundation which crumbles away at once at the touch of History.

(i.) *The Bible.*

For when we ask, " What is the Bible and whence came it ? How was this library of history, poetry, and letters bound together in one whole ? Who decided which books or letters should be included in it, and which of the many contemporary documents should be omitted ? " the answer is inevitable. The Church formed the canon of Scripture. The Church decided which books should be included. The Church gives it all the authority it has. It is the Church's record of her experience. For many years the first Christians lived on the oral teaching of the Apostles, without any book at all except the Jewish scriptures, with occasional circular letters from some of the Apostles. Then, as the time came for the Apostles to pass away, the Church adopted four accounts of our Lord's life which embodied their witness. To these she added a journal of the first activities of the chief Apostles, which preserved a picture of the primitive life of the Church : these were supplemented by such letters as were believed to have been written by the Apostles, or best to represent their teaching ; also by the book of Visions in which is enshrined the later witness of St. John. These make up the New Testament, the purpose of which is to preserve the witness of the Apostles, and to provide us with a touchstone and a test capable of correcting any deviation from the original deposit of the Faith. The Bible is the Church's Book, which she alone can interpret. The New Testament was not written for, or addressed to, the unconverted. It presupposes a certain atmosphere of the Church's Tradition. It was written for those who " continued stedfastly in the Apostles' teaching and fellowship, in the breaking of bread, and the prayers " (Acts ii. 42). Every one for

whom these biographies were written, and every one to
whom these Epistles were addressed, was a baptized
and confirmed Churchman living in communion with
his Bishop, and had been thoroughly instructed in the
faith, discipline, traditions, and worship of the Church.
To take this Book and treat it as a book of magic from
which each person, whether baptized or not, and however
uninstructed, can evolve a religion of his own, is a tragedy
of superstition which has split Christendom into a thousand fragments, and has created an individualistic
religion of self-will which is in clear contradiction to the
Gospel. For when we ask how the merits of Christ's
Sacrifice are to be applied to the individual soul, or how
each person is to be caught up into the Atonement and
made " at one " with God, the witness of History is
clear.

(ii.) *The Holy Catholic Church.*

The last action of our Lord in the great work of the
Atonement is to make men " at one " with one another
by incorporating them into His Body, the Church. There
is no such thing as an unattached Christian who belongs
to no body, no Church, no communion or fellowship. I
have met men who have boasted that they were Christians
belonging to no Church or sect, but standing alone with
Christ. Their lives were free from ordinary vices and
they freely used the language of Protestant piety. But
in every case they were hardened in spiritual pride, that
most deadly sin of religious men ; and it was obvious
that without knowing it they belonged to the sect of the
Pharisees, the Separatists. They were simply the prey
of that fundamental falsehood which lies at the root of
so much of the sin and misery in the world, the atomic
conception of personality, which treats each person as a

separate isolated solitary unit, a self-contained or self-sufficient individual. This is the most bitter fruit of Protestant teaching, which has brought world-wide ruin on the Christian world. It lies behind all the issues of this great War which is wrecking our civilization, a war of ideas in which Luther's principles, wrought out to their logical conclusion in the philosophy of Nietzsche, are in direct conflict with the teaching of Christ. This Individualism is the curse which has blighted our civilization by making the anti-Christian principle of Individualism and of unrestrained competition, as opposed to the Christian principle of co-operation, the basis of our social and economic life. It has inevitably produced our vast inequalities in the distribution of wealth, our miles of deadly slums, our national sins of that "covetousness which is idolatry," and of a soul-destroying luxury. It is deeply ingrained in the minds of Englishmen as well as of Prussians. And if this fundamental heresy is not uprooted and torn away from the mind, there is no hope for the world. For this selfish Individualism is the very essence of Sin ; and Sin, when it is perfected, *must* bring forth death. If after the war the nations still base their life on this evil principle of unrestrained competition, it is only a question of time for us to await the inevitable consequences of sin at the root of our social life, and to see again the whole world plunged in a universal war.

Again, this evil principle of Individualism, of the atomic conception of personality, lies behind all the divisions of Christendom which has split it into a thousand fragments : and all talk about reunion is hopeless until this conception has been uprooted from the minds of men. As long as men think of themselves only as separate individuals whose religion is between their soul and God alone, and believe what they like, and go where they like, and do what they like, so long the religion of Christ is impossible. For Christianity is essentially corporate ; and Individualism is the religion of Cain, who, with hands still reeking in his brother's blood, flings his challenge to God and man, " Am I my brother's keeper ? "

So, if we are to learn the last action in the great process of the Atonement by which Christ uplifts each one of us into union with Himself in order that He may make us " at one " with God, we must grasp the fact that there is no such thing as individual salvation apart from the Body of Christ, the Church ; and that our redemption is primarily and essentially corporate, the incorporation into a body.

The Church which Christ founded is not an accidental by-product of His teaching, but the essential purpose of His coming. The Way of Salvation is not primarily individualistic, but corporate. The Church is not human in its origin, but divine. The Church is not constituted by the assembly of individual Christians, but individuals become Christians by being baptized into the Church. The Church is not a club of converted men who agree to worship together, but a family of the twice-born sons of God who have been incorporated into a fellowship by a creative act of God when they were born again of Water and of the Spirit in Holy Baptism. The Church is not merely an assembly of converted individuals, each complete, self-contained, and rounded off, like a bag of marbles ; not like a bunch of steel filings, each drawn to a magnet ; not like a mob of persons united only by a common purpose. She is not merely an organization, but an organism : not a partnership which can be made or dissolved at will, but a family relationship dependent on a common birth and on the circulation of a common life. The Church is a Body. Each member of the Church is as one of those millions of little cells which make up our body, having each a life of its own which can only be realized by spending itself on the common life of the whole. The Church is a family, a brotherhood which is bound together, not by the accident of mutual agreement, but by the necessities of a common birth, and by the circulation of a corporate life.

Why did our Lord choose this method of a corporate salvation, of salvation by incorporating man into a body, instead of the method of individual salvation by attaching men one by one to Himself, as units without any vital connection with one another ? Is it not clear that His is the only way of saving man from sin ? For the essence of sin is Selfishness. If man is to be delivered from sin he must be saved from selfishness. If a converted man were left in isolation, how would he be educated in unselfishness, self-sacrifice, and love ? The convert must be incorporated into a Brotherhood, in order that by the discipline of fellowship he may correct his faults, and may learn to find his life as he loses it in the larger life of the whole.

The soul can only be saved, the personality can only be developed by uplifting it into the fellowship of a larger life which will encompass it, sustain it when it is weak, correct it when it is wrong, educate it by calling out all its capacity for self-sacrifice, chivalry, and love, and satisfy all its needs with the perpetual inflowing of a purer and richer life. And this larger personality which embraces and encompasses man's soul and interpenetrates it with a love which identifies that soul with Himself is the Living Christ; and the Church is His Body. So in the early Christian writings we find no suggestion of a merely individual salvation. Many of the first converts to Christianity in Judæa must have heard the preaching

of St. John the Baptist, and of our Lord, and of His
Apostles ; and they would remember that one message
ran through the whole of that teaching, the message of
corporate salvation, the Gospel of a Kingdom. This
was the message, ringing with ever growing intensity
through the writings of the Old Testament, to which the
first Christians listened at every Eucharist—the coming
of the Messiah, who was to redeem the race and the world,
and to establish the Kingdom of God. And the message
of the Old Testament was summed up in the vision of
Daniel :—" in the days of those kings shall the God of
Heaven set up a Kingdom which shall never be destroyed."
" I saw in the night visions, and behold there came with
the clouds of heaven one like unto a son of man, and He
came even to the Ancient of days, and they brought
Him near before Him. And there was given Him
dominion, and glory, and a kingdom, that all the peoples,
nations, and languages should serve Him : His dominion
is an everlasting dominion which shall not pass away,
and His Kingdom that which shall not be destroyed "
(Dan. ii. 44, vii. 13, 14). This was the message of St. John
the Baptist :—" Repent ye, for the Kingdom of Heaven
is at hand " (St. Matt. iii. 2). This was the message of our
Lord Himself :—" Jesus came into Galilee, preaching the
Gospel of God, and saying, The time is fulfilled, and the
Kingdom of God is at hand : repent ye, and believe in the
Gospel " (i.e. the good news) (St. Mark i. 14, 15). This was
the commission He gave to His Apostles :—" and He sent
them forth to preach the Kingdom of God " (St. Luke ix. 2).
This was the absorbing subject of His last instructions
to His Apostles in the forty days after His Resurrection
when He spoke to them of " the things concerning the
Kingdom of God " (Acts i. 3).

And this Kingdom was presented to the first Christians

in the letters of the Apostles as the Bride of Christ (Eph. v. 25, 29 ; 2 Cor. xi. 2) ; and the Body of Christ (Eph. i. 22, 23 ; Col. i. 18 ; Rom. xii. 4, 5 ; 1 Cor. xii. 12). Nowhere do we find the least hint of that modern heresy of an individual salvation apart from incorporation into Christ's Body the Church. When men convinced of sin cried out, "Brethren, what shall we do ? " St. Peter answered, "Repent ye, and be baptized every one of you in the name of Jesus Christ unto the remission of your sins ; and ye shall receive the gift of the Holy Ghost " (Acts ii. 37, 38). When persons try, from the teaching of St. Paul in his Epistle to the Romans, to establish a new method of salvation by faith alone, apart from Church and Sacraments, they seem to forget that every one of those to whom that letter was addressed was a baptized, con-firmed, and communicant member of the Church. And when they urge that conversion alone, or faith in our Lord alone, are sufficient for salvation, they seem to forget that the very Apostle upon whose writings they base this false teaching, after being thoroughly converted, was thus bidden :—"Arise, and be baptized, and wash away thy sins, calling on His name " (*ibid*. xxii. 16). If ever there was a case in which individual salvation apart from Church and Sacraments might have seemed possible, it would have been the conversion of St. Paul. But we find the Apostle of Faith most insistent on the corporate life and the outward form—seeking Holy Baptism for the washing away of his own sins ; laying on his hands in Confirmation (*ibid*. xix. 6); and proclaiming the central importance of the Holy Eucharist by declaring that God had given to him a special revelation of its institution (1 Cor. xi. 23).

The Bible knows absolutely nothing of the selfish religion of " I won't have anyone between my soul and God." This religion, which tries to create a sort of spiritual

vacuum in which an isolated soul may hold communion
with God apart from " the communion of saints," is the
deadly heritage of the false philosophy of atomic personality, and finds no support at all in the Bible. In
the earthly life of our Lord, He repudiates this deadly
heresy by seeking the sympathy of His Apostles (St.
Mark xiv. 34), by accepting the ministry of an Angel
(St. Luke xxii. 43), and by holding communion with
the saints (*ibid.* ix. 30). And St. Paul, the Apostle of
Faith, knows nothing of this religion of a spiritual vacuum.
He knows only of the religion of the Body of Christ.
" For in one Spirit were we all baptized into one body."
" The Body is not one member, but many." " Now ye
are the body of Christ, and severally members thereof "
(1 Cor. xii. 13, 14, 27). " For I say, through the grace
that was given to me, to every man that is among you,
not to think of himself more highly than he ought to
think ; but so to think as to think soberly, according as
God hath dealt to each man a measure of faith. For
even as we have many members in one body, and all
the members have not the same office : so we, who are
many, are one body in Christ, and severally members one
of another " (Rom. xii. 3–5). " And let the peace of
Christ rule in your hearts, to the which also ye were
called in one Body " (Col. iii. 15).

If, then, we are sufficiently convinced that our salvation is not primarily individual but corporate, that Christ
saves us by incorporating us into His Body the Church,
we may now go on to consider how a man may enter
fully into the power of that great Atonement which God
has provided. And in this we may take St. Paul and
St. John for our guides.

CHAPTER VII

MAN'S RESPONSE

WE have seen in a former chapter that the Atonement is supernatural and co-operative, that it is an act of God which calls for a response from man. What is to be man's response?

1. REPENTANCE

It is probably true to say that perfect penitence can be offered by our Lord alone. For His sinless soul alone can know the full loathsomeness of sin : He, being one with the Father, alone knows what sin costs the Heart of God : He, being one with man, alone can offer God a perfect contrition poured forth from the unsullied purity of His broken Heart. It is to be noted as one of the many witnesses to His Deity, that He Who has brought conviction of sin home to the hearts of millions of men is Himself entirely unconscious of any personal guilt. Every saint has been a penitent whose penitence only deepens as he draws closer to the Heart of God. With us, the shadows deepen as we draw nearer to the Light ; but He Who dwelt in uninterrupted communion with the Father is entirely unconscious of any personal sense of guilt. The sins of the world which He took into His Heart when He made Himself "at one" with man found in Him no response at all. And so He, and He alone, can take them away. The suggestions of Satan, "the prince of this world" who wrestled with Him in the Garden of Gethsemane, failed to evoke the faintest quiver of acquiescence or consent in His human will. "The prince of this world cometh and hath nothing in Me" (St. John xiv. 30). Satan's power to hypnotize entirely failed. His mesmerism did not work, and the spell is broken and his power is shattered. The representation of man as surrounded by a magic circle which only the sign of the Cross can break is counted by many as merely a mediæval superstition; but it possibly preserves this truth, that Satan's power was shattered by our Lord's death upon the Cross.

Since, then, Christ alone can offer an ideal penitence, it is for us to see how Christ in us helps us to repent. And for this we may take St. Paul as our guide.

(i.) *Conviction of Sin, and Contrition.*

Repentance begins with Conviction of Sin. Conviction of sin generally begins with attrition: and this must deepen into Contrition. Attrition is sorrow for sin from fear of the consequences. The Prodigal Son was first moved to repentance by seeing that sin fails to bring satisfaction; famine — "in want" — slavery — "I perish" — were the first movements of conviction of sin. Only as he drew nearer home did the thought of what his sin had cost the father's heart come home to him. Attrition is the sorrow of slaves; contrition is the sorrow of sons. Contrition is sorrow for sin because it pains the heart of someone who loves us. A little boy used to be punished when he did wrong; but being an obstinate little fellow who did not mind pain, punishment never did him any good. He used to put his ears back, and resolve to "do it again" when he had the chance. But one day, as his mother was dressing for dinner, he cuddled up to her, and said how much he loved her. She said, "You can't really love me, or you would do what I told you to do." He looked up and saw tears in his mother's eyes. These sacraments of sorrow revealed to him for the first time that his sins pained the heart which he loved and which loved him, and he went away and wept bitterly ; and nothing would induce him to sin again in that way. He was contrite. After Conviction comes Contrition. After Contrition comes Conversion.

(ii.) *Conversion*.

Conversion is the reversal of the will so that it now hates and loathes what once it chose to do. It is the shifting of the centre of one's life from self to God. Or again, it may be the awakening to sonship which realizes its relationship to God. It involves the disentangling of the will from its connection with a misdirected past, and the redirection of the will into responsive harmony with the Will of God.

But the will is a very complex activity of our personality ; and if we are to know the peace which passeth all understanding, and enter into the full riches of the Atonement, Christ must heal the will. For a divided will is one of the effects of sin, and is destructive both of peace and of power. Without falling into that error of psychological analysis which would pigeon-hole the various movements of our personality and label them as separate faculties, we may, for convenience' sake, thus analyse the divided will. A naval lieutenant once told me that he enjoyed his hot bath so much that he couldn't get out of it when he ought to do so, until he had turned on the cold tap ! This shows us the divided will with three separate activities which we may call the fundamental will, the will of desire, and the executive will. His fundamental will was to do his duty, what he ought to do. This remained steadfast ; but it was counteracted by

(Rom. v. 8). The prevenient love of God is one of the deepest riches of His mercy. While Saul is still persecuting Him, hurrying with blinded heart and eager feet along the road to Damascus, the living Christ is patiently waiting, encompassing him with His long-suffering love. The Hound of Heaven follows on his tracks, and will not abandon him. Those goads, those pricks of the conscience, which maddened blinded bigotry into frenzy, were the strivings of the Holy Spirit, the yearning pleadings of the Christ. In the long years, when absorbed in self, we were cold and irresponsive and indifferent to God ; His love encompassed us, and waited when perhaps we were in flaming rebellion against His Holy Will, and spat venom and contempt and scorn into His Face. When " we crucified the Son of God afresh and put Him to an open shame " (Heb. vi. 6), the Living Christ still patiently loved us, and our Great High Priest still kept on saying, in His intercession before the Eternal Throne, " Father, forgive them, for they know not what they do." When there was nothing in us to attract the love of God, everything to repel ; when we did not want Him, would not have Him ; when, full of vanity, we fluttered like moths round the bewildering, fascinating, glittering lights of the world, or wallowed like swine in the lusts of the flesh ; when, bewitched and bewildered by the pleasures of sin, drawn hither and thither by our lusts and passions, we lay bound and helpless beneath the spell of Satan, paralysed, unable even effectually to desire to be holy ; when hope was dying and love was dead ; then the strong Son of God would not forsake this treacherous soul, but clove His way with wounded Hands and bleeding Heart through all the snares of Satan until He had broken the spell, and caught up the soul in the arms of His mercy, and, breathing on it the warm breath of His love, had fanned

the dying embers of faith and hope and love into a faint
desire for Him which will grow into a true repentance.
It is in union with the living Christ that conviction,
contrition, and conversion reach their full fruition. As
the Lord turned and looked on Peter with the eyes of
deep disappointment which revealed His wounded love,
so He turns and looks on you and me. The Passion is a
present reality, not merely a past event. The Sacred
Heart of Jesus never changes. He loves you as much as
He loved St. Peter or St. John. "Jesus Christ is the
same yesterday, to-day, and for ever" (Heb. xiii. 8).
Yesterday denied by Peter ; to-day, disowned by those
who shrink from confessing Him because they fear a
mocking taunt, His Heart bleeds afresh. Yesterday
His back torn by the bloody scourge in Jerusalem ; to-
day bleeding from many a cruel wound in the trenches
of France and Gallipoli. Yesterday crucified on Calvary,
and listening to the polished scorn of Sadducee or the
thoughtless ribaldry of the mob ; to-day crucified afresh
in London, and listening to the subtle sarcasm of literary
unbelief, or the careless blasphemy of the multitude.
Wherever His loved ones suffer, whenever His loved
ones sin, the Sacred Heart of Jesus feels it. We hear the
careless jest in a West End club about some fallen woman ;
but astride that prostrate form we see the Champion of
the weak and oppressed with eyes of flame pointing to
the seducer, and hear the thunder of that voice of the
King rolling down the ages, "Inasmuch as ye have done
it to one of the least of these My brethren, ye have done
it unto Me " (see St. Matt. xxv. 40). Jesus cannot cease
to suffer because He will not cease to love. To us, then, who
have been baptized into Christ, and are made " at one"
with Him, the glorious Atonement brings with it a fathom-
less conviction of sin. Look at Him ! He chose you,

H

watched over you, incorporated you into His very life. He lives in you. He hoped great things from you. He wants you to help Him to redeem the world. He wants your lips through which to proclaim the everlasting Gospel, and to convert the nations. He wants your hands with which to do His works of mercy. He wants your heart as a sacred shrine for the fire of His love. In spite of this high calling we have turned aside to the love of the world, and of the flesh, and to the service of the devil. What must be the disappointment of that sensitive Heart ! If the tears in the eyes of a mother can move a son to repentance, see the tears in the eyes of Jesus, and offer to Him a broken and a contrite heart.

(iv.) *Detachment and Attachment.*

Two processes mark a true repentance ; first, Detachment and then Attachment. The will must be torn away from that to which it clings, self or sin or the world, and must be attached to God. The temporal consequences of sin are knit up into the mechanism of time and space, and cannot be undone, though their developments may be overruled by God, Who knows how to bring good out of evil. This fact that these effects of sin are beyond our control will explain why penitence is an abiding attitude of the forgiven soul, the undertone of every holy life. What should be our attitude towards these consequences of our sin which are beyond our control ? St. Paul teaches us that with regard to the past we have a twofold duty :—to remember and to forget.

Remember—because, although through God's mercy our personality is disentangled from the sin and our sin is pardoned, yet the evil may still bear fruit, and we are the cause of it.

Remember—in order that we may exalt God's mercy.

When "the snares of death compassed me round about and the pains of hell gat hold on me," the Lord "delivered my soul from death ; mine eyes from tears and my feet from falling" (Ps. cxvi. 3, 8).

Remember—that we may be humble and patient under those hindrances and disabilities which still remain in our soul as the effect of sin on human faculty. The penitent is a convalescent.

Remember—in order that we may be humble in our attitude towards God, and gentle, pitiful and forbearing in our judgment on the frailty of our brethren.

Remember—that our love may never grow lukewarm.

So St. Paul again and again recalls to the minds of his converts the memory of his sin, "how that beyond measure I persecuted the Church of God, and made havock of it" (Gal. i. 13).

"Give the world joy, but patience to the Saints.

> Saints did I say ! with your remembered faces,
> Dear men and women, whom I sought and slew !
> Ah ! when we mingle in the heavenly places
> How will I weep to Stephen and to you !
>
> Oh, for the strain that rang to our reviling,
> Still when the bruised limbs sank upon the sod,
> Oh, for the eyes that looked their last in smiling,
> Last on this world here, but their first on God."

But while it is our duty to remember, it is also our privilege to forget. God does not forgive by halves. He forgives altogether when He forgives at all. So the Apostle bids us forget ; "But one thing I do, forgetting the things which are behind, and stretching forward to the things which are before, I press on toward the goal unto the prize of the high calling of God in Christ Jesus" (Phil. iii. 13, 14).

Forget—in order that no doubt may dim the joy of

reconciliation or shake our faith in the fact that Christ
has won the full pardon of our sins for us.

Forget—in order that no brooding thoughts of the
shame of the past may weaken the courage with which
we face the future.

Forget—for fear lest in useless brooding over the past,
Satan may yet again weave his webs around the soul
which gazes on the decaying corpse of pardoned sin.

(v.) *Confession and Absolution.*

When our contrition is really deep, it will find utterance in a frank confession ; and this confession will not
seek to minimize our faults, or to avoid the full shame
of our sin. Christ has done for us what we could not do
for ourselves. He has borne the guilt of our sin. But
we can bear the shame. " Be not ashamed concerning
thy soul. For there is a shame that bringeth sin : and
there is a shame that is glory and grace. . . . Be not
ashamed to make confession of thy sins " (Ecclus. iv. 20,
26). Pride is the very root of sin ; and to confess one's
sins to the Church represented by God's priest is the best
way to break our pride and win humility. And is this
not also a due to the Body of Christ, the Church ? For
we have seen that our salvation is not primarily individual,
but corporate. We are saved by being incorporated into
the Body of Christ, the Church. Our sins are not a matter
between our souls and God alone. When we sin we
injure the Body of Christ ; and a true repentance will
seek God's pardon in that Body which sin has injured.
Just as the social sins of one member bring sorrow and
shame to a family, a regiment, or a nation, so all sin,
even the most subtle and hidden, does injury to the
Body of Christ, the Church, the Communion of Saints.
When one cell in your body becomes diseased, it spreads

corruption all around it, and must be healed or expelled. No body of any sort could exist at all unless it had powers of self-discipline, power to say on what conditions persons can be admitted to its fellowship, power to regulate its life, power to judge who may be admitted to, and who should be repelled from, its communion. It is so with every organization, club, college, benefit society, regiment; it is so with every organism, flower, animal, human body, family, nation, and church. All have their method of admitting, assimilating, disciplining the material which is woven up into their life, and of expelling that which cannot be assimilated. When our Lord founded His Church to be His Body through which He would teach and act and work out the world's redemption, He gave it just these powers of initiation, communion, and excommunication or cutting-off from communion. We have not only the record of the great commission to forgive or retain sins (St. John xx. 22, 23), but we see this power in actual operation. St. Paul writes to the Corinthians: "But to whom ye forgive anything, I forgive also: for what I also have forgiven, if I have forgiven anything, for your sakes have I forgiven it in the person of Christ; that no advantage may be gained over us by Satan: for we are not ignorant of his devices" (2 Cor. ii. 10, 11); "holding faith and a good conscience: which some having thrust from them made shipwreck concerning the faith: of whom is Hymenæus and Alexander; whom I delivered unto Satan, that they might be taught not to blaspheme" (1 Tim. i. 19, 20). Or in another case: "And ye are puffed up, and did not rather mourn, that he that hath done this deed might be taken away from among you. For I verily, being absent in body but present in spirit, have already, as though I were present, judged him that hath so wrought this thing, in the name of our Lord Jesus,

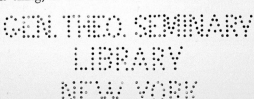

ye being gathered together, and my spirit, with the power of the Lord Jesus, to deliver such a one unto Satan for the destruction of the flesh, that the spirit may be saved in the day of the Lord Jesus " (1 Cor. v. 2–5).

How is it possible for those who teach a merely individual salvation, and declare that their sins are a matter between their souls and God alone, and profess to base this false teaching on the writings of St. Paul himself, to ignore this witness of St. Paul to the corporate discipline of the Church ? Is not this to do the very thing against which Scripture warns them, to take his epistles and wrest them, " as they do also the other scriptures, unto their own destruction " (2 St. Peter iii. 16)? It is useless for them to say that human judgment in confession may err : for they themselves also are human, and the expectation of human error is far greater when a sinner judges himself, than when he submits his case to the judgment of the Church by making his confession.

We have briefly sketched in barest outline the way in which union with our Lord deepens conviction and contrition, and leads the sinner to confession. We do not confess our sins to inform God of what we have done. He knows this already. He saw us do it. He heard us say it. We own our sins in order that we may disown them. Our will is entangled with our past and associated with our sins. We confess our sins in order that we may publicly dissociate our will from them. We announce in our confession that we now abhor that to which once we consented. And when we kneel to confess our sins to God in His Church with deep contrition and a strong purpose to amend, and a living faith in Christ, God forgives us for His sake, and we are made " at one " with God.

The joy of the Absolution which the priest pronounces

in God's name is that it delivers us from the doubt and uncertainty which must always accompany any merely subjective movement of our own soul. When our assurance of pardon in the precious Blood of Christ rests only on the witness of our own heart, we may, and often do, deceive ourselves. "The heart is deceitful above all things" (Jer. xvii. 9). Again, a merely subjective assurance of pardon is at the mercy of our temperament, and emotions, and fluctuating states of mental and physical health.

But when the penitent seeks God's pardon through that ministry of reconciliation which Christ Himself appointed for the remission of sins, his assurance rests not merely on the feelings of his own deceitful heart, but on the authoritative pronouncement of the Church which has judged his repentance and believes it to be sincere. Thus Christ speaks through His Church : " Our Lord Jesus Christ, who hath left power to His Church to absolve all sinners who truly repent and believe in Him, of His great mercy forgive thee thine offences ; And by His authority committed to me, I absolve thee from all thy sins, In the Name of the Father, and of the Son, and of the Holy Ghost." (See Book of Common Prayer, *The Visitation of the Sick*). Thus God in His Church pardons the penitent and admits him to communion. The inner witness of the soul is thus reinforced by objective sanctions ; and assurance is strengthened by the judgment of the Church, the authoritative pardon, the support of fellowship, and the grace of absolution.

In an earlier chapter we have seen that our at-one-ment, reconciliation, reunion with God must be both supernatural and co-operative, must come from above and work from within. It must be supernatural, for no powers of nature can restore what sin has destroyed. It must be co-operative with the energy of a living faith, for no gift of God can benefit us unless by faith we assimilate it and make it our own.

2. Faith

What is Faith ? Faith is not superstition. Superstition is belief based on sentiment and ignorance, and has no moral value whatever. Faith is not credulity, the readiness to believe anything. Credulity is belief based on insufficient evidence, and is quite without moral value. Faith is not acquiescence, the thoughtless acceptance of inherited creeds which have never been appropriated or made our own.

(i.) *Trust and Self-Surrender.*

Faith in its first movements is trust in a Person : and in its fullness Faith is entire self-surrender to that Person. Faith is not merely a moral conviction, or an intellectual approval. It is an activity of the whole personality. It has in it an element of intellectual appreciation ; it has in it a movement of emotional affection ; but its central energy is a movement of the will surrendering itself in perfect trust to Jesus. And this act of central self-surrender has three leading characteristics—obedience, trust, and love. This is the co-operative activity of the soul which enables it to appropriate the gift of God, and to be caught up into the power of the Atonement.

It may seem to be passive ; but it is really active in its self-restraint. A man is drowning, and the deep waters are threatening to swallow him up. He is caught in the grip of a strong tide which is bearing him downward to certain destruction. His own strength is exhausted. He cannot save himself. In answer to his cry for help, a strong swimmer plunges into the river, and

cleaves asunder the water, and the drowning man hears a
voice in his ear, " Do as I tell you. Don't cling to me.
Lie still and trust me." He obeys, and lies still in the
hand of the strong swimmer who supports him. But
what an energy of will is needed to conquer the instincts
which impel him to cling to his rescuer ! What an
intense activity of self-restraint the passive attitude of
self-surrender demands from him ! So our self-surrender,
which looks to Christ alone to accomplish our deliverance,
is a real energy of our soul.

And how does He uplift us into the power of His
Atonement ? By making us " at one " with Himself.
By identification. By incorporating us into His life that
we may dwell in Him and He in us. Being " reconciled
to God through the death of His Son," we shall " be saved
by His life " (Rom. v. 10). We are caught up into union
with a larger Personality, which not only interpenetrates
us through and through, but encompasses us all around.

In the first place, in Christ " we have our redemption
through His Blood, the forgiveness of our sins" (Eph.
i. 7). "There is . . . now no condemnation to them that are
in Christ Jesus " (Rom. viii. 1). The haunting memory
of a sinful past is dead. The stings of a guilty conscience
no longer torment. The terrors of Judgment no longer
pursue. He has borne it all for me, on my behalf, instead
of me. He has done for me what I could not do for myself.
He has borne the guilt. He has satisfied the law of righteousness. In Him we are pardoned, acquitted, forgiven,
free. Let us accept it with life-long gratitude. Do not
let us doubt it. This was " the joy that was set before
Him " for which He "endured the cross, despising the
shame " (Heb. xii. 2), to embrace us in the arms of His
mercy, to cleanse us from our sins.

And not only " in Him " is the guilt of sin done away,

but also " in Him " the power of sin is broken, the spell of Satan is shattered. We are " delivered out of the power of darkness, and translated into the kingdom of the Son of His Love " (Col. i. 13). All that the poor emaciated slave feels when rescued from the torture of cruelty, the chains, and filth of a slave dhow, and safe on the deck of a British battleship, all this the devil-haunted soul finds when it awakens " in Him." But not only pardon, forgiveness, freedom, and peace are found in Him.

(ii.) *Re-creation.*

" In Him " again we find the miracle of a newly created personality. "Wherefore if any man is in Christ, he is a new creature : the old things are passed away ; behold, they are become new " (2 Cor. v. 17). Sin blinds the mind, hardens the heart, weakens the will, destroys the very power of the soul to love the good. Just as the very tissues of the body are destroyed by sulphuric acid, so the central power of the soul for faith and hope and love is destroyed by sin. And " in Him " it is created anew. But in using these metaphors and similes of destruction and re-creation drawn from the bodily life to illustrate the death and disintegration and restoration of the soul, we must remember that they are necessarily imperfect ; we know so little of what personality is and of the real nature of the soul. It may help us to realize their meaning if we see the process of redemption in actual working. I once asked Father Dolling what was the secret of his power to reclaim the " hopeless cases " which were so often sent to him when everyone else had abandoned them,—broken-down drunkards, and most abandoned criminals ; and he said, " There is only one way to redeem them. I try to live inside them by love and sympathy, and to do for them what they cannot do for themselves. They have ceased to love or respect themselves. I love them and reverence them because they are dear to the Heart of Jesus. They have ceased to trust themselves because they know how often they have tried and failed, and proved themselves untrustworthy. I trust them, and take my chance of failure ; because that is the only way in which they can be made trustworthy again. They have lost the power to hope for themselves. They feel that their character is fixed, and they do not expect to be better. So I hope for them and in them ; and gradually hope dawns again in their heart." He then sent for a doctor, who was what the world would call a hopeless drunkard and thief and had been abandoned by all his friends, and said to him, " I want you to show Father Bull the town, and to get me two shillingsworth of stamps," and gave him half a sovereign. When the doctor went to get his hat, Father Dolling explained to me, " Of course he may fail me. But I must take my risks. He can only be made trustworthy by somebody trusting him. And I feel sure that I shall not be deceived." How different from the cold, calculating, cast-iron methods of the unforgiving world ! How true to the methods of God, Who trusts us when He knows that we are untrustworthy, and so at last makes us worthy of trust ! "For while we were yet weak, in due season Christ died for the ungodly. . . . God commendeth His own love towards us, in that, while we were yet sinners, Christ died for us " (Rom. v. 6, 8). How beautiful to see these poor sinners encompassed around and embraced in the all-penetrating sympathy of that great servant of God, so that the dead soul who had lost the power of faith and hope and love is brought back again to life by the love which drew all its power from the Sacred Heart of Jesus, and sought and saved the lost ! This is what we mean by the creative love of Christ, Who quickens into life that which is dead in our souls, and makes all things new. "God chose the foolish things of the world that He might put to shame them that are wise : and God chose the weak things of the world that He might put to shame the things that are strong : and the base things of the world, and the things that are despised did God choose, yea and *the things that are not*, that He might bring to nought the things that are " (1 Cor. i. 27, 28).

3. STRENGTH

The characteristic note of the new life in Christ, now that "in Christ we are a new creature ; the old things are passed away ; behold, they are become new," is the gift of strength. We note the change from the cry of helpless weakness to the cry of triumphant strength. "What I hate, that I do. . . . The good which I would I do not : but the evil which I would not, that I practise " (Rom. vii. 15, 19). "My grace is sufficient for thee : for my power is made perfect in weakness " (2 Cor. xii. 9). "I can do all things in Him that strengtheneth me " (Phil. iv. 13). Ours is not merely the Gospel of a good example which would only have filled us with despair. It is a Gospel of "Power from on high." It is a fundamental mistake to reduce the grace of God to a mere assurance of God's good will toward us, as it was in the Old Testament. To Christians grace is not merely an expression of a will : it is the communication of a life. Atonement is not the alteration of a mental attitude, but an incorporation into the Divine Humanity. "For the Law was given by Moses ; Grace and Truth came by Jesus Christ " (St. John i. 17).

them to their work (Acts xiii. 2, 4), directs their efforts (*ibid*. xvi. 6, 7) and edifies, or builds up, the Church (*ibid*. ix. 31). The treatment of the Atonement as embracing the whole process of the "one-ing" of God and man is of course open to the criticism that we are mentally confusing justification with sanctification. But we would plead that we are anxious to escape from the scientific abstractions of theologians into the free movements of life in its fullness. Just as psychology was hindered in its development as long as men clung to the abstractions of "heart" and "mind" and "will," each separated off into a water-tight compartment, and could make no progress until men recognized that these were only labels for the convenient treatment of various activities of personality ; just as physical science invariably misses the truth when, having legitimately made an abstraction for the purposes of study, it treats this abstraction as though it were the reality ; so theologians may quite legitimately make an abstraction, for the purposes of study, between justification and sanctification. But the truth of the Atonement lies in the whole of that process of Identification by which God makes man " at one " with Himself. It is a loss of proportion and a real schism when some teachers so emphasize St. Paul's doctrine of justification by faith as to underrate his teaching on the Church, and pit his letters to the Romans and Galatians against his letters to the Colossians and Ephesians which possibly represent his own correction, in the light of later experience, of the misunderstanding of his teaching in the earlier letters. Not only must we take all St. Paul's teaching as a whole, but we must remember also that St. Paul was not the only Christian, and that his experience of Christ needs to be supplemented and corrected by the experience of St. John. Three fatal schisms mar the work of many theologians on the Atonement. They used to separate the Three Persons of the Ever-blessed Trinity, and construct a whole system of legal bargaining between the Father and the Son. They separate Christ from His Church in such a way as to underrate the Sacraments. And they separate the individual soul from the Body of Christ, the Church, in such a way as to underrate the Sacred Ministry. This is the very spirit of schism in the very heart of unity, of " at-one-ment." We shall best appreciate the work of the Holy Spirit in the Atonement if we sum it up in the words "The Holy Spirit comes not to supply an absence, but to accomplish a Presence." For this He brooded over the Blessed Virgin Mary, that Christ might be born within her ; and thus He broods over the Church and the waters of the font to give in Holy Baptism the new birth of water and of the Spirit to each soul which is, by this means of Grace, incorporated into Christ. As He descended on our Lord in His Baptism to abide within His sacred Humanity, so in Confirmation He comes to take up His abode within us. As the Body of Christ was " conceived by the Holy Ghost," and as He "through the Eternal Spirit offered Himself without spot to God" (Heb. ix. 14), so at every Eucharist it is by the operation of the Holy Ghost that the bread becomes the holy Body of Christ, and the wine His precious Blood, and that our Lord, both Priest and Victim, presents again His Sacrifice to the Father. In the words of the Scottish Liturgy we pray :—

" We beseech Thee, most merciful Father, to hear us, and to send Thy Holy Spirit upon us, and upon these Thy gifts and creatures of Bread and Wine, that being blessed and hallowed by His life-giving power they may become the Body and Blood of Thy most dearly beloved Son, to the end that all who shall receive the same may be sanctified both in body and soul, and preserved unto everlasting life."

This brings us to one last thought on the Atonement. " In Christ " we have not only union with God, but also union with one another in the bonds of that Holy Communion which none may receive alone.

We must try to grasp the splendour of God's will and purpose, which is not to save us as single isolated individuals, but to knit us together in one body so that at last redeemed mankind may fulfil the purpose of his creation, and with one heart and mind offer to God with ceaseless praises a reflection of Himself. Christ saves us by incorporating us into a fellowship, a body. In a family the soul first finds that discipline which weans it from selfishness, and offers it the opportunities of ministry, self-sacrifice, and love. Then, in a larger circle than the family, consider what a change comes over some slouching lad who has been destroying himself by self-will and self-indulgence when his life is incorporated into a regiment. He is caught up into a larger personality, even though it be artificial ; he is encompassed around by a larger life than his own, which interpenetrates him with its influences and redeems him from selfishness. He learns obedience, so that self-will is disciplined into the readiness for self-sacrifice. He learns comradeship, so that he is ashamed not to share his life with a chum. He has a past ; not the discreditable past of his individual life, but the great traditions of his regiment. He recognizes corporate responsibility and knows that the credit of the regiment is in his keeping ; until at last the corporate life has done its work, and educated what was once a mean little soul to forget himself and tread gaily the heights of heroism. So in this present war we have seen the life of a Nation beating in the hearts of three million of our best and

CHAPTER VIII

THE REUNION OF CHRISTENDOM

SO our thoughts on the Atonement, the "one-ing" of God and man, have led us up to the Altar where in the Communion of the Church Christ incorporates us into Himself in order that He may make us "at one" with the Father. In baptizing us into His life and communicating to us His Body and Blood, He incorporates us into His sacred Humanity. And in this sacred fellowship of the Communion of the Body and Blood of Christ, we have the bond which alone can bind together the Body of Christ, the Church. "The cup of blessing which we bless, is it not a communion of the Blood of Christ? The bread which we break, is it not a communion of the Body of Christ? Seeing that we, who are many, are one bread, one body: for we all partake of the one bread" (1 Cor. x. 16, 17).

1. OUR LORD'S PRAYER

We may fitly bring these meditations on the Atonement to a conclusion by trying to see what we can do to hasten the fulfilment of our Saviour's dying prayer that we may be one. "Neither for these only do I pray, but for them also that believe on Me through their word; that they may all be one: even as Thou, Father, art in Me, and I in Thee, that they also may be one in Us: that the world may believe that Thou didst send Me. And the glory which Thou hast given Me I have given unto them; that they may be one, even as We are One; I in

them, and Thou in Me, that they may be perfected
into one : that the world may know that Thou didst
send Me, and lovedst them, even as Thou lovedst Me "
(St. John xvii. 20–23). All who love the Lord Jesus in sin-
cerity and truth must try to win the answer to His prayer
in the Reunion of Christendom. We know how His
Heart must feel the scandal of our unhappy divisions
which hinder the coming of His Kingdom, and the conversion of the world. What can we do to hasten the
fulfilment of His Heart's desire ?

There are many signs that the time is approaching
when this Reunion will become possible. Just as in days
of old the Roman Empire unconsciously prepared the
way for the coming of Christ and the spread of the
Gospel, so to-day many forces are working together to
unify the race. We see the signs. The triumphs of
science which have annihilated time and space so that
each morning the whole world knows what has happened
in the remotest corner of the Universe, the international-
ization of science, medicine, and scholarship, the inter-
penetrating effect of commerce, travel, and emigration,
the commingling of races in new lands, all these are—or
ought to be—educating us out of our insularity, and,
without weakening national sentiment, cultivating the
habit of international thought. Even this awful war
in which we are engaged may be something more than
the death agony of a selfish civilization ; it may be the
birth pangs of a new sense of brotherhood.

2. Reunion with the Church Expectant

A vast process of education is going on which is touch-
ing deeper motives than science or commerce can touch.
Every morning, as we read our paper, our hearts sob for
the sorrows of Belgium and Serbia. We see with infinite

pity the people of France mourning amidst the ruins of their cathedrals, the stately shrines of a thousand years of sacred memories. We follow along the icebound roads the long weary procession of the peasants of Poland and of Russia, homeless and ruined, limping away broken-hearted to an unknown destiny. We die side by side for the same cause. Hand in hand the flower of the youth of France, Russia, Italy, Belgium, Serbia, and Britain are passing through the Veil by thousands day by day, and awakening in the unveiled Presence of Jesus their Lord and King, whom now they see face to face and know even as they are known. And even our enemy, who may seem to us at present, because of the deliberate and culti-vated atrocities with which he has made war, a leper unfit to mix with his fellow men, a maniac possessed with many devils, comes within the compassion of the Sacred Heart of Jesus, who still knows how to cleanse the leper, and to cast out the devils, and to restore a nation to its right mind. These lads who have watched one another worshipping on earth at separate altars are of necessity united in the worship of Paradise before the Throne of God and of the Lamb. So that not only is the war dis-solving prejudice by teaching us to try to know and under-stand one another, but it is forcing us to attend to that blessed reunion beyond the Veil. Does not this point to the first true step towards the Reunion of Christendom? We must not try to hasten the day when we may worship at one altar on earth by those unhappy common com-munions which are based on a profound insincerity, a pretence that we who are divided are at one. This seems to be an attempt to escape from the consequences of our sins without the pain of a true repentance. We cannot hasten the Reunion of Christendom by methods which, if they are persisted in, will certainly split our Church in

two and erect new barriers between ourselves and reunion
with the Russian and the Roman Churches. When we ask
with passionate eagerness, "Lord, dost Thou at this time
restore the Unity of Christendom?" our Lord still
answers, "It is not for you to know times or seasons
which the Father has set within His own authority."
But as we mingle our tears and prayers with those of
other nations, as we weep by the grave-side of all
who have died for their country, our Lord points on to
the first step toward reunion. By the revival of prayers
for the departed, by veneration of the Saints and Martyrs,
we may seek reunion with the Church in Paradise and in
Heaven. On this all Bible Christians will agree : for this
union in the communion of saints is the prevailing note
of Christian worship in the Bible. God is the God of
Abraham, of Isaac, and of Jacob, not the God of the dead
but of the living, for all live unto Him (St. Matt. xxii.
32 ; St. Luke xx. 38). As we run our race we are surrounded by a great cloud of witnesses, and we "come
unto Mount Zion and unto the city of the living God,
the heavenly Jerusalem, and to innumerable hosts of
angels, to the general assembly and Church of the first-
born . . . and to the spirits of just men made perfect"
(Heb. xii. 22, 23). The departed are only hidden from
our sight ; they are not separated from our communion in
Christ. He is "the Head over all things to the Church,
which is His Body, the fulness of Him that filleth all in
all" (Eph. i. 22, 23). Again and again in the visions of
the Book of the Revelation the first Christians were
taught to mingle in worship with the Saints and
Martyrs before the Throne of God and of the Lamb.
And Saint Cyril of Jerusalem thus describes the communion of the early Church (i.e. about A.D. 370): "Then
we make mention too of those who have fallen asleep,

first of the patriarchs, prophets, apostles, and martyrs, that God would at their prayers and intercessions receive our supplication : then, too, on behalf of our holy fathers and Bishops and briefly of all amongst us who are fallen asleep before us, believing that it will be the greatest benefit to the souls on behalf of whom supplication is offered, while the holy and most awful Sacrifice is lying before us " (St. Cyril, *Lectures on the Mysteries*, v. 9). Until prayers for the departed and the veneration of the Saints and holy Martyrs have become a normal part of our devotions, the Church in England cannot hope to fulfil her vocation of mediating reunion between the millions of Christians in the Russian and the Roman Church. For neither of those parts of the Holy Catholic Church would hold communion with a Church which shamefully neglects its departed (as we at present do), and which so utterly fails to hold communion with those beyond the Veil. But if reunion with the Church in Paradise and Heaven is the first step toward reunion in the Church on earth—for the new Jerusalem does not work up from below, but descends " out of Heaven from God "—the second step seems to be to correct our faults of character and temperament, and to cultivate a large vision of the truth. So many of the misunderstandings which separate us seem to spring not only from the gross sins of pride, ambition and self-assertion on one side and the other, but also from a lack of appreciation of the many-sidedness of Truth. When we see one aspect of the truth, we are tempted to treat it as the whole ; and the assertion of one aspect seems to lead to the denial of other visions of the Truth. But in this we are not true to the Catholicity of the Bible or to the ideal of the Church. We must clearly see that it is unity, *not uniformity*, after which we are to strive.

3. The Catholic Ideal

The ideal of the Catholic Church is not that of a bullet-mould, but of a flower garden : not uniformity, but diversity in unity. As in the very Being of the Godhead we find the splendours of Deity revealed in the inter-action of three Persons, so in the Catholic Church we can only hope to reflect the light of God truly by pre-serving the full activity of each soul at its highest power. The Catholic Church must not aim at the uniformity of the barrack square, but at the unity of a family. As we never knew what kinship existed between our earth and the sun until the one white light of the sun had been split up into its many colours in the spectroscope, so we shall never learn the full richness of the Truth of God until it has passed through the prism of many minds. Is not this one true motive of missionary enthusiasm ? Each nation and each race has some new splendour of the love of God to reveal, as the Gospel shines through the heart of the gentle Hindu, the facile Japanese, and the steadfast Chinaman. So each one of us in his measure, according to his race and nation, his age and generation, his character and temperament, is able to reflect some new richness of the love of God : and the Church is a diamond with many facets, each reflecting a different ray of the one light. And surely the way to work for unity is patiently to go on correcting those imperfect ideas which lie behind all our divisions. Is not this the secret of the Catholicity of the Bible ? The Truth of God is passed through the medium of many minds. The historical accuracy of St. Luke is supple-mented by the mystic insight of St. John. Both are true, but different aspects of the truth as it is passed through the medium of varied human experiences. If

we cultivate the habit of correcting our prejudices and trying to understand how truth appears to men of different education, experience, and temperament, shall we not contribute something towards removing obstacles to the reunion of Christendom ?

We must remember that the vast majority of Christians who are living in separation from the communion of the Catholic Church still belong to her by reason of their baptism. Without in the least weakening the absolute claim of the Catholic Church on the allegiance and obedience of all men, we must find some method by which we can fully and thankfully recognize the reality of the individual spiritual experience of Nonconformists without in any way condoning their separation. For to ignore the sin of separation from the Apostolic Fellowship, the communion of the Catholic Church, would be to condemn Christendom to endless anarchy, and to frustrate our Lord's prayer that we all may be one. And to deny a spiritual experience which has been so fruitful in holiness of life and self-sacrifice and missionary zeal would be to blaspheme against the Holy Ghost. Believing, then, that most Nonconformists by their Baptism belong to the Body of Christ, the Holy Catholic Church, but are separated from her communion by sins and misunderstandings on both sides in days gone by, may we not work hopefully for reunion by trying to remove misunderstandings and to appreciate their point of view ? If we cannot conquer their prejudices, we can at least try to conquer our own by the steady endeavour to see many aspects of the Truth.

Shall we not win the fullest vision of truth of which we are capable amidst the clash of contraries, which are not necessarily contradictories ? Instead of hardening differences into divisions, we must learn to distinguish

without dividing. Instead of allowing them to harden into contradiction, we must learn to harmonize the soul and body of religion, the mystical and the historical, the corporate and the individual, the spiritual and the institutional, the static and the dynamic.

Applying this principle to the subject of our meditation, let us see our Lord and Saviour Jesus Christ, the Son of God, in varying visions on different planes of thought.

4. Varying Planes of Thought

We see first the vision of the Eternal and the Temporal. Seated in heavenly places, we watch the procession of the ages winding up the Mount of God ; and everything is seen under two aspects—as an event which happens in time, and as a process which has an eternal activity.

We think then of Birth in concentric circles of Reality, all of which centre round the manger cradle at Bethlehem :— the Birth of the Universe, the Body of God, and the Cosmic Christ, the Word of God. " All things were made by Him ; and without Him was not anything made that hath been made. . . . He was in the world, and the world was made by Him, and the world knew Him not . . . And the Word became flesh, and dwelt among us " (St. John i. 3, 10, 14). "For in Him were all things created, in the heavens and upon the earth, things visible and things invisible, whether thrones or dominions or principalities or powers ; all things have been created through Him, and unto Him ; and He is before all things, and in Him all things consist. And He is the Head of the Body, the Church : Who is the beginning, the first-born from the dead " (Col. i. 15, 16). We notice in these two passages how naturally St. John and St. Paul pass from the Cosmic to the Historical and the Ecclesiastical planes of thought. We too may pass

from the birth of the Universe to the cradle of Bethlehem, and worship Him Who "for us men and for our salvation came down from heaven, and was incarnate by the Holy Ghost of the Virgin Mary, and was made Man." Then, passing to another plane of thought—the Ecclesiastical— we see the birth of His Body the Church on the day of Pentecost—the Body through which He will teach and energize, working out the world's redemption. St. Paul, as we have seen, was always insisting on this, the corporate aspect of the Christian life, both in his earlier and later Epistles. But again we follow Birth on to another plane of thought ; passing from the Ecclesiastical to the Sacramental, we rejoice in our Baptism wherein we were born again of Water and Spirit, buried into the Death of Christ, and rising into His Life, so that we dwell in Him and He in us. And this vital union with the living Christ is not dependent on our subjective feelings and emotions, which fluctuate with our state of health and spiritual progress. Regeneration, our spiritual birth, is an act of God which is of necessity as independent of our will as is our natural birth. But the strong assurance of the truth of the sacramental system need not lead us to underrate the joyful realization of what God has done for us, when we awaken to sonship and respond to the gift of grace, and, on the plane of the mystical, know birth after birth of the life of Christ within us as in heart and mind and will we are conscious of " the arousal of a holy thing," the life of Christ awakening within us and bringing us into harmony with the Whole, the rhythm of the Universe.

And all these aspects of Birth are gathered up in Eucharistic worship, as in the first action of the Holy Sacrifice we present our Bread and Wine and Water to God at the Altar where flowers breathe, and candles burn,

and incense ascends. Man as the High Priest of all creation gathers up the songs of birds, and the scent of flowers, and the shining of the stars ; and unites with thunderings and lightnings and the four living creatures and the four and twenty elders in singing the song of Creation which greeted the Birth of the Universe " when the morning stars sang together, and all the sons of God shouted for joy " (Job xxxviii. 7 ; see also Rev. iv., v.).

The Song of Creation.

" Holy, Holy, Holy, is the Lord God, the Almighty, which was and which is and which is to come. . . . Worthy art Thou, our Lord and our God, to receive the glory and the honour and the power : for Thou didst create all things, and because of Thy will they were, and were created " (Rev. iv. 8, 11).

It may be said that in thus speaking of Birth we are only playing with words, and confusing thought by mingling facts with metaphors in a bewildering confusion. We admit that this method of concentric circles of Reality and different planes of thought lacks precision. But is not this a great gain ? We cannot be sure that a truth is divine unless we fail to understand it exhaustively. Truth which is capable of being snipped up, and docketed, and put in pigeon-holes is a dead truth. The living truth is greater than man's mind : and Mystery is the only shrine of ultimate Reality. As long as we are entangled in the mechanism of Time and Space, and can only think through the imperfect instrument of the brain, and are obliged to use words if we want to speak at all, so long do we know that our expression of Divine truth must be imperfect, and all language about the spirit, human or divine, must be metaphorical. We can only learn Divine truth in worship.

So we pass on from Birth to consider the Passion and Death on varying planes of thought, in concentric circles which all centre round the Cross of Calvary.

On the Cosmic plane we listen to the groaning and the striving of the Universe disordered by man's sins and eagerly waiting for redemption. "The earnest expectation of the creation waiteth for the revealing of the sons of God . . . the whole creation groaneth and travaileth in pain together until now" (Rom. viii. 19, 22). The cosmic aspect of the Passion leads us to contemplate the sufferings of the poor animals who, especially in this awful war, "with us bear the burden and heat of the day" as having a place in the great redemption. For no sparrow falls to the ground without our Father (St. Matt. x. 29). Animals which can weave their way so wonderfully into our life, and become so dear to our hearts, will surely find a place in the fountain of Love, the Heart of Jesus. After contemplating the cosmic aspect of the Passion in which Christ suffers in all the Universe which He upholds and which only consists in Him, we pass on to see the Passion in its historic manifestation and its consummation on the Cross. This has already been before us : so we may proceed to look at the Passion in its Ecclesiastical aspect. The Church of God, the Body of Christ, betrayed by false Apostles and sinful priests ; bound by the fetters of the State : blindfolded by prejudices : struck and spat upon by unbelievers : forsaken by the faint-hearted : crucified by those who owe her a loyal obedience ; crowned with the thorns of intellectual bewilderment ; bleeding from the wounds of our sinful divisions ; brokenhearted but undefeated, Christ in His Church treads again the Way of Sorrows which is the path of victory. A church which knows no sorrows and does not bear the scar of many a wound could not be recognized as the Body of Christ.

We pass from the Ecclesiastical plane to see the Passion on the plane of the Sacramental, as day by day it is shown forth in every land from ten thousand altars when the holy Body is broken and the precious Blood outpoured. " For as often as ye eat this bread and drink the cup, ye proclaim the Lord's death till He come " (1 Cor. xi. 26).

Passing from the Sacramental to the Mystical plane, we have already seen how by sin we " crucify the Son of God afresh and put Him to an open shame," because by love He has identified Himself with us. There are other mysteries of Death known to the Mystic, such as the Dark Night of the Soul, of which it is impossible to speak. They lie very near to the heart of the mystery of Evil and to the redeeming purposes of God. Abram knew it when the " horror of great darkness " fell upon him, and he learned the future of his race (Gen. xv. 12). Moses knew it amidst the thunderings and lightnings of Sinai when he " drew near to the thick darkness where God was " (Ex. xx. 21). Job knew the land " where the light is as darkness " (Job x. 22). The Psalmist knew it as the deep waters flowed over his soul, and the enemy persecuted his soul. " He hath smitten my life down to the ground : he hath made me to dwell in dark places, as those that have been long dead " (Ps. cxliii. 3). He knew it also as the abiding-place of God Who has " made darkness His hiding-place, His pavilion round about Him." " Clouds and darkness are round about Him : righteousness and judgment are the foundation of His throne " (*ibid*. xviii. 11 ; xcvii. 2). The prophets and the Apostles knew it : and our Lord often speaks of that " outer darkness " which He tasted for us in the dereliction on the Cross. All souls know it who come into close contact with the mystery of Evil. Its mysteries defy description, but the death of hope and the chill touch of despair may form one element in it. For some it may possibly be described as the death of self-reliance which is necessary before we can be raised in Christ. We know that we can pass through this darkness with Christ holding our hand. "He that followeth Me shall not walk in the darkness, but shall have the light of life." "I am come a light into the world, that whosoever believeth on Me may not abide in the darkness" (St. John viii. 12; xii. 46). Every aspect of Death on every plane of thought is summed up for us in the second action of the Holy Eucharist, when our Bread and Wine, by the overshadowing of the Holy Spirit, become the Body and Blood of our dear Redeemer. As we plead His Death before the Father, we mingle with that great multitude of the Redeemed which no man can number, of every nation and tribe and kindred and people, who have washed their robes and made them white in the Blood of the Lamb; and we learn the sweet new song of our Redemption. "Worthy art Thou to take the book and open the seals thereof: for Thou wast slain, and didst purchase unto God with Thy Blood men of every tribe, and tongue, and people, and nation, and madest them to be unto our God a kingdom and priests." "Worthy is the Lamb that hath been slain to receive the power, and riches, and wisdom, and might, and honour, and glory, and blessing." "And every created thing which is in the heaven, and on the earth, and under the earth, and on the sea, and all things that are in them, heard I saying, 'Unto Him that sitteth on the throne, and unto the Lamb, be the blessing, and the honour, and the glory, and the dominion, for ever and ever'" (Rev. v. 9, 10, 12, 13). Thus the Song of Creation becomes the Song of Redemption in the adoration of the Lamb Who has conquered Sin and Death and Satan.

After meditating on Birth and Death on various planes of thought, it only remains to think thus of Life, and we shall have followed the process of the Atonement to its rich consummation. Knowing nothing of the ultimate nature of Life, we can only speak of it vaguely. On the Cosmic plane we know that Christ, the Word of God, is the life of the Universe. When once we are fully conscious of our ignorance, we shall not dare to exclude even that which at present seems to us inanimate from the realm of Life. The interplay of attraction and repulsion which holds the stars together, and which unites the tiniest molecules in chemical affinity, since it is an expression of the Will of God, may be the earliest dawn of love ; and love is life. We recognize more easily the life in fish and flower and animal because they are in the line of our ancestry. And all that lives lives only in Him, Who is "the Word of Life" (1 St. John i. 1). We follow the upward procession of life from the unconscious, through the conscious, to the self-conscious : from the determinate, through the indeterminate, to the self-determinate : from the physical, through the intellectual, to the moral and spiritual : from the temporal to the eternal.

We pass from the Cosmic to the Historical, and "the Life was manifested, and we have seen, and bear witness, and declare unto you the Life, the eternal Life, which was with the Father, and was manifested unto us" (*ibid.* i. 2). "And the witness is this, that God gave unto us eternal life, and this life is in His Son. He that hath the Son hath the life ; he that hath not the Son of God hath not the life" (*ibid.* v. 11).

We pass from the Historical to the Ecclesiastical and Sacramental, and note that Christ lives and labours in His Body, the Church, as our Great High Priest. We see Him clothed in priestly garments moving amidst the

candlesticks, guiding and overruling the Church's life
as the Shepherd and Bishop of our souls (1 St. Pet. ii. 25).
It is He Who baptizes every infant : it is He Who offers
every Eucharist : He Who absolves the penitent : He
Who proclaims the living and life-giving Word.   When
the Church fails, it is because we—His Body—will not
respond to the demands of His Spirit ; and often now,
as in the days of old, Christ sits by the well of living
waters, and is weary with His journey, as some priest
or parish or nation refuses to respond to His call.
As our Great High Priest He proclaims Himself, "I am
the first and the last, and the Living One ; and I was
dead, and behold I am alive for evermore, and I have
the keys of death and of Hades " (Rev. i. 18).   Passing
then to the Mystical plane of thought, we find in Him
that union of the soul with God which is Eternal Life.
All that the mystic means by that sense of peace and
harmony with the Whole, the One in All and All in One,
when his soul seems to rise into perfect unison with the
rhythm of the Universe, is summed up for us in the writings of St. Paul and St. John.   " For ye died, and your
life is hid with Christ in God " (Col. iii. 3), " that Christ
may dwell in your hearts through faith ; to the end that
ye, being rooted and grounded in love, may be strong to
apprehend with all the saints what is the breadth and
length and height and depth, and to know the love of
Christ which passeth knowledge, that ye may be filled
with all the fulness of God " (Eph. iii. 17–19).   This is
the At-one-ment, the Gospel of Identification, by which
God through infinite suffering makes man at-one with
Himself.   It is to be uplifted into reunion with the Heart
of God, the Ever-blessed Trinity, caught up into that
eternal interpenetration and reaction of Love.   " He
that hath My commandments, and keepeth them, he it is

that loveth Me : and he that loveth Me shall be loved of My Father, and I will love him, and will manifest Myself unto him. . . . If a man love Me, he will keep My word ; and My Father will love him, and We will come unto him, and make our abode with him " (St. John xiv. 21, 23). And this brings us to the last action of the Holy Sacrifice in the Eucharist when, after we have shown forth the death of Christ before the Father, Christ comes in His risen life to bestow on us His Body and His Blood. He comes not as a disembodied spirit to inspire us, but in the full richness of His divine Humanity to dwell within us, "that we may dwell in Him and He in us." And then in union with Him we are presented to the Father and " accepted in the Beloved." This is the fulfilment of the Atonement and Eternal Life. For Eternal Life is never presented in the Scriptures as a future reward, but always as a present possession—the state of the soul which is " at one " with God through Christ. Not " this shall be," but " This *is* life eternal, that they should know Thee the only true God, and Him Whom Thou didst send, even Jesus Christ " (*ibid*. xvii. 3). " He that heareth My word, and believeth Him that sent Me, hath " (not "shall have ") " eternal life, and cometh not into judgment, but hath passed out of death into life " (*ibid*. v. 24). " For this is the will of My Father, that every one that beholdeth the Son, and believeth on Him, should have eternal life ; and I will raise him up at the last day." "He that eateth My Flesh and drinketh My Blood hath eternal life : and I will raise him up at the last day. For My Flesh is meat indeed, and My Blood is drink indeed. He that eateth My Flesh and drinketh My Blood dwelleth in Me and I in him " (*ibid*. vi. 40, 54–56).

We have now followed the great process of the Atonement to its fulfilment in a life of abiding communion with the living God.

To every man upon whom is laid the necessity to preach the Gospel and to tell of the unfathomable mysteries of God's Love and Suffering and Holiness, there must come deep conviction of sin as he sees himself and his sins and his base ingratitude in the light which shines from the Cross, and knows how often he has crucified the Son of God afresh and put Him to an open shame.   But we preach not ourselves, but " Christ crucified."

> Standing afar I summon you anigh Him,
>   Yes, to the multitudes I shout and say,
> "This is my King ! I preach and I deny Him,
>   Christ ! Whom I crucify anew to-day."[1]

If we look at ourselves in the light of His love we shall wither away in despair at the depth of our failure, our sin and our shame, our selfishness, our lukewarm love. But this would be to rob Him of His victory. We have failed and fallen into sin only because we did not abide in Him.   However loathsome we may be in our own sight, however deep our self-contempt, still if we will look away from ourselves and gaze up into His Face and, humbling our pride, be content to owe all to Him, we shall know that His Sacred Heart never changes, and that He Who loved the leper can still love us.   " Hereby shall we know that we are of the truth, and shall assure our heart before Him whereinsoever our heart condemn us ; because God is greater than our heart, and knoweth all things " (1 St. John iii. 20).   Our assurance is in Him, not in ourselves.   He only asks that we shall leave ourselves, and come to Him.   " Come unto Me all ye that labour and are heavy laden, and I will give you rest."

[1] " S. Paul," F. W. H. Myers.

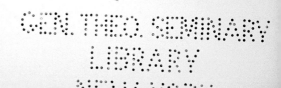

"And him that cometh to Me, I will in no wise cast out"
(St. Matt. xi. 28 ; St. John vi. 37).

"For if, while we were enemies, we were reconciled to
God through the death of His Son, much more, being
reconciled, shall we be saved by His life ; and not only
so, but we also rejoice in God through our Lord Jesus
Christ, through Whom we have now received the reconciliation" (Rom. v. 10, 11).

> "This hath He done, and shall we not adore Him ?
> This shall He do, and can we still despair ?
> Come, let us quickly fling ourselves before Him,
> Cast at His feet the burthen of our care,
>
> Flash from our eyes the glow of our thanksgiving,
> Glad and regretful, confident and calm,
> Then through all life and what is after living
> Thrill to the tireless music of a psalm.
>
> Yea, thro' life, death, thro' sorrow and thro' sinning
> He shall suffice me, for He hath sufficed :
> Christ is the end, for Christ was the beginning,
> Christ the beginning, for the end is Christ."

PRINTED IN GREAT BRITAIN BY
WM. BRENDON AND SON, LTD., PLYMOUTH.